Contents

Authors' foreword **2**

D1535560

North American Edition

Copyright © 2016 text AG&G Books

The right of A. & G. Bridgewater to be identified as authors of this work has been asserted by them in accordance with the Copyright, Designs and Patents Act 1988.

Copyright © 2016 illustrations and photographs IMM Lifestyle Books

Copyright © 2016 IMM Lifestyle Books

Designed and created for IMM Lifestyle Books by AG&G Books. Copyright © 2004, 2016 "Specialist" AG&G Books

Design: Glyn Bridgewater; Illustrations: Gill Bridgewater and Coral Mula; Editor: Fiona Corbridge; Photographs: AG&G Books, Ian Parsons, Builder Center, Marshalls and Do It All.

Current Printing (last digit)

10 9 8 7 6 5 4 3 2 1

Printed in Singapore

Patios: Designing, building, improving and maintaining patios, paths and steps is published by Creative Homeowner under license with IMM Lifestyle Books.

ISBN: 978-1-58011-750-0

Creative Homeowner®, www.creativehomeowner.com, is distributed exclusively in North America by Fox Chapel Publishing Company, Inc., 800-457-9112, 1970 Broad Street, East Petersburg, PA 17520.

Authors' foreword

What could be better, on a warm summer's day, than to relax on the patio with family and friends. A patio gives you somewhere pleasant to read a book, talk quietly, play with the children, cook on the barbecue, watch a water feature and go to sleep on a chaise lounge – all wonderfully therapeutic, quality-time experiences that everyone should enjoy. And then when the sun goes down in the evening, you can switch on some soft lights and music, and invite neighbors round for a party. Have you ever noticed that when people are on a patio, away from the confines of the house and the formalities observed in indoor spaces, they are generally more relaxed and expansive? They smile and laugh, make bigger movements with their hands, stride around and tend to behave in a less inhibited way. It is almost as if the great outdoors is our natural habitat – perhaps it is!

So there you have it – this is the age of the garden room. No more hiding away indoors: now is the time to build the biggest and best room in the house – the patio. This book will guide you through all the stages of designing, planning and building. Now is the time to turn your patio dreams into patio reality.

About the authors

Alan and Gill Bridgewater have gained an international reputation as producers of highly successful gardening and DIY books on a range of subjects, including garden design, ponds and patios, stone and brickwork, decks and decking, and household woodworking. They have also contributed to several international magazines.

IMPORTANT NOTES

Many of the procedures for the projects are potentially hazardous. Read through the following notes and take safety precautions.

Safety while building
Some procedures are inherently dangerous, such as lifting heavy weights, or working with an angle grinder or cement mixer. The best advice is to take your time, and whenever possible work with a friend. Children are drawn to building work, attracted by the chugging of a cement mixer or piles of wet mortar. Allow them to watch and help with simple tasks, but always be on your guard.

Electrical safety
Weather and electricity power cables are not natural allies: water, rain and morning dew on the lawn all pose a hazard. Always use a safety electrical circuit breaker between the power source and the machine.

Assessing your garden

A successful patio relies on achieving a balance between your requirements and the character of the garden. Almost every garden is big enough for a patio, and even in the tiniest yard, you can go a long way to modelling the space to make a comfortable 'room' open to the sky. The first step is to spend time in your garden, deciding what you require from a patio. Look at the space, talk through how you want to use it, and then make plans to fulfil these aims.

Will my garden be big enough? How do I start?

MAKING PLANS

When you have looked long and hard at your garden, assessed its size and character and decided on the scope and style of the patio, work out how to set the whole plan in action.

Let's say that your garden is on a slope and you want to build a brick patio close to the house. Are you going to bring in material to level out the slope and create a flat area for the patio? Or are you going to move the existing earth around to make a terraced area? Will new ground levels mean that you have to adjust the height of your fences? If the new patio means you will be sitting at a higher level, will this impact upon your privacy or that of your neighbors? Do you have to consider the position of existing drains, or build drains to take water away from the patio? Think about all the implications of going ahead with the project, and ways to deal with them.

GARDEN SIZE

Take the size and shape of your garden, your needs and budget into account, and plan out the patio.

Decide how much space you are prepared to relinquish to the patio. If you are preparing for retirement, you might opt for a large, low-maintenance patio with easy-to-manage raised beds. If you have young children, your priority might be a safe, enclosed space for them to play in. If you delight in eating outdoors, you might prefer a patio close to the house. If you are aiming for a retreat where you can read, a private space well away from the house might appeal.

A diminutive courtyard garden that has been levelled and paved with pale, light-reflecting tiles. Metal containers help to bounce light and also glint attractively. A slim strip of earth has been preserved as a border.

GARDEN STYLE

Tucked away in a walled garden, bricks and cobbles have been used to draw a bold semicircle.

Just like the rooms in your home, the style of the patio should be planned to suit your lifestyle and needs. However, the choice you make will to a great extent be dictated by the form and age of your house, the shape and size of your garden and, of course, your own particular likes and dislikes.

If you want privacy, it doesn't make much sense to build raised decking that puts you in full view of your neighbors. If you have teenage children, a barbecue might be a popular feature. If you enjoy sleeping out of doors, a patio with low lights, a covered area and bunk beds would be great fun. If you have always fancied a hammock, incorporate a couple of posts into your patio. Decide how much time you want to dedicate to construction, think about possible materials (stone, brick, concrete or wood) and then choose a style that will look good in the established surroundings.

A decking patio with seaside overtones – matching raised beds are topped with decorative turquoise crushed stone.

Choosing a patio, path and steps

What will be the best option for my garden?

There are hundreds of ways to make a patio, and many materials to choose from. A stone patio could be made of real cut stone slabs, reconstituted stone slabs, crazy-paved stone, crushed stone, stone set on edge, or stone plus brick. There are also brick patios, wooden decking patios, and patios made from gravel, bark or sawdust. Alongside your patio you may need paths and steps. Whatever the size of your garden, there will be an exciting option for you.

TYPES OF PATIO

Basic patio
Plain and functional

→ The specifications of a basic patio are that it is a simple shape, with little detailing. It might consist of an area of plain cast concrete, or be made up of plain concrete slabs, gravel, brick, or even bark. However, the shape will be rectilinear, and there will be no changes of level or decorative edgings. For any patio, the expense and expertise involved depend on the amount of detail in the design, so a basic patio is both inexpensive and relatively easy to build. (See page 24.)

Decorative patio
Patterned and detailed

↗ A decorative patio is both functional and visually dynamic. Unlike a plain patio, the design attempts to use materials in a stimulating way. Plain paving stones are exciting in their own right, but set alongside cobbles, they can create magic! (See page 36.)

Decking patio
The beauty of wood

↗ Decking can be made of anything from planks of rough-sawn timber to wood that has been planed, molded and pressure-treated with preservatives. (See page 34.)

Avoiding slippery surfaces

A slightly rough surface to decking material can be an advantage to counteract slippery surfaces. Especially if your wood patio is in a shady area where algae or moss can grow on its surface.

OTHER PATIO OPTIONS

Natural patio ~ This is a patio that imitates nature. If we define a patio as a dry, level area that is fairly comfortable underfoot, a natural patio could therefore be made from gravel or sand to resemble a beach, from pine needles to reflect a forest floor, from shale to mimic a mountainside, or from long grass to look like a meadow. (See page 30.)

Salvaged mixed-media patio ~ A patio made from a mixture of salvaged materials such as old tiles and bricks, railroad ties, sawdust or tree slices – any safe, salvaged materials that can be put down to make a level area.

Raised or sunken patio ~ Patios that are set either above or below ground level. An old, unused swimming pool can be covered over and turned into a wonderful patio by installing heating, bubbling fountains and exotic plants. (See page 38.)

High-tech patio ~ A patio that uses modern materials such as stainless steel, copper sheet or glass bricks to create a surface that draws inspiration from industrial materials.

TYPES OF PATH

You must consider cost, suitability and ease of handling. Bricks are expensive, but fairly light in weight. Reconstituted stone slabs are cheaper, but very heavy. Purpose-designed pavers (super-hard, thin concrete or clay bricks) offer another possibility. Think about the decorative potential of various materials, work out how you will lift the individual units, then make your choice.

Bricks are the perfect option for a traditional country cottage garden.

Modern reconstituted stone slabs are both functional and decorative.

A design of bricks combined with pavers can look really striking.

Crazy paving is low in cost and made from small pieces of stone.

A selection of different types of real stone makes an unusual patio.

Decking tile paths can be purchased in kit form, making construction easy.

TYPES OF STEPS

Brick and stone steps
A traditional option for a cottage garden

← Brick and stone steps are a favored choice because not only are the materials reasonably low in cost and easy to handle, but the design possibilities are endless. A good, easy-to-build option for steps is to use bricks for the risers and side walls, and stone crazy paving for the treads.

Wooden steps
Inexpensive and easy to construct

A wide, low fight of steps with railroad tie risers and stone shingle treads.

Slow-rise decking steps leading to a decking patio – good for a sloping site.

PATIO ADDITIONS

When the patio is finished, you can start to consider additional features and furnishings for it. Think of the patio as a garden room, just like a room in your house, to which you can add various items to make it more comfortable, user-friendly or attractive.

Depending upon the climate in your area and the situation of your house, you might need shelter from the wind, and a pergola with a plant canopy to keep off the sun. Will you be using the patio at night? If so you may need lighting or heating. Which family requirements do you need to cater for? Perhaps you'd like a barbecue, a large table for family meals, a sand corner for the toddlers, or a bed for the dog. Do you want storage space? You might fancy erecting a hammock – will you need to put in posts to hang it from?

Do you want planters or raised beds for plants, or a small herb garden? Do you want to incorporate a gently trickling water feature? Live in the new garden room for several weeks before you make any hard and fast decisions.

A raised bed made from a reconstituted stone kit makes a beautiful addition to a reconstituted stone slab patio.

A traditional Japanese feature – water gently dribbling into a stone basin – would enhance a natural patio.

Checking the site

Before you start work, check the site to make sure that there aren't any practical factors that are going to cause difficulties. You need to consider everything, from the position of underground drains to overhead cables, the way the sun affects the site at different times of day, shadows cast by trees, where a power supply will run from – anything that might cause trouble. Draw up a hit-list of potential problems and make sure that they aren't going to hold you back.

SITE CHECKLIST

Stand on the proposed site and look slowly around you. Look at the house, the trees and the position of the sun. Assess the degree to which the patio is overlooked by adjoining houses.

Sun and shade ~ Study the position of the sun at times when you are likely to use the patio. You will probably want to avoid heavy shade, and you need to think about how to deal with full sun – it might be too strong to sit in, so you may wish to counter it by providing a shaded area, such as under a pergola, or buy garden furniture to do the job.

Scale, orientation and viewpoints ~ Walk around the garden in order to view the site from a good number of positions. Do you want to see the patio from indoors? Do you want it to be an open, public space or a secluded spot, on high or low ground?

Providing shelter ~ Most patios need shelter – from the sun and wind, for privacy and for planting. If you live in an unpredictable climate, a covered area to provide shelter from light showers might be a good idea.

Problems above and below ground ~ Avoid a site that is crossed by underground service pipes for drains and electricity. If there are overhanging trees, will they drip on you? Keep away from tree roots, because they might cause concrete to crack.

Soil type and digging ~ Dig a few test holes to check whether or not it is possible to build on that site. If there are old concrete foundations, an old pond, wet areas or pockets of sand, these may cause difficulties and the design of the patio may have to be modified accordingly. A site on wet clay will be a lot of hard work to dig, so you may prefer to choose a site that requires less digging.

PRESERVING PRECIOUS TOPSOIL

If you are going to move a lot of soil or lay down a concrete slab, you have to avoid burying the fertile topsoil, which is the layer plants need to grow. As you strip away the topsoil, put it to one side. Shovel the sterile subsoil on to an area that needs to be built up. Finally, bring the topsoil back to the site and spread it over the subsoil.

GROUND CONDITIONS AND PROBLEMS

If the ground in the proposed site is overly boggy, sandy or rocky, there is a risk that the conditions will in some way be a nuisance – either while the work is in progress or when the patio has been completed. It is usually possible to overcome these problems, but sometimes it is simpler to opt for another location, or to build a raised patio that doesn't require digging.

THINGS TO CONSIDER BEFORE STARTING TO BUILD A PATIO

Overlooking buildings
Avoid siting a patio in full view of neighboring houses, unless you want to be an exhibit.

Overhanging trees
Too many overhanging trees can be a problem – dripping after rain, dropping sticky fruit etc.

Proximity to a road
If the road is very busy, avoid noise and fumes by building the patio on the other side of the garden.

Degree of exposure
It is good to have a view, but is the site too breezy, or exposed to driving rain?

Shade
Most people like a patio to have plenty of sun, but is there enough shade?

Septic tank
If your garden has a septic tank, build the patio well away from it to avoid the nuisance of odor, flies or overflow.

Designing a project

Once you have decided on the type of patio – size, style and location – it is most important to draw out a plan and make design notes on paper. When all the facts are set out, you will be able to do calculations to work out quantities of materials required. This written record of specifications will always be ready to refer to throughout the project – useful when contacting suppliers, and essential during the construction process.

Do I really need to draw designs?

Inspirations

Get yourself a folder complete with plain and gridded paper, pencils, a ruler and colored crayons. Make a "wish list" of things you would like to have. If the design includes brick and stone, decide on colors and textures. Don't be too specific at this stage, just try to visualize the overall shape, color and form. Start a scrapbook of pictures that inspire you (do not limit the collection: include everything at this stage).

YOUR CONCEPT

You may know that you want to build a patio by the house rather than a patio at the end of the garden, but are you aware of the available materials, colors and textures? Talk the idea over with your family and friends, perhaps even with your neighbors.

VISUALIZING

Cover the ground with something the same size as the envisaged patio, such as a tarpaulin. Live with this full-size plan for a few days and see how it impacts on your use of the garden. Could it be bigger? Does it need to be realigned? Set out tables and chairs and try it out – does it feel right?

DESIGN CONSIDERATIONS

Look closely at your chosen materials in order to balance their dimensions with the proposed structure. If, for example, you are building a rectangular brick patio, the starting point for the design will be the surface pattern you would like, and the width and length of the patio in terms of whole bricks. It is much better to spend extra time at the design stage to avoid problems later.

DRAWING YOUR DESIGN

↗ *Use graph paper to ensure an accurate plan, which will help you assess how the proposed position of the patio will relate to the house and garden.*

Measure your garden and draw the plan to scale on graph paper, so that each square is a set measurement. Draw the patio on the plan so that its position is distanced from a couple of fixed points, such as the house and a boundary fence. If you are building a structure from manufactured materials (bricks, slabs or blocks), draw out the various views. As far as possible, size the structure to use whole units, and minimize complex cutting.

Checklist

- Is the design suited to the size and character of your garden?
- Have you worked out the exact dimensions?
- Do these need to relate to unit sizes?
- Have you chosen the best materials at the lowest cost?
- Is the design structurally sound?
- Do you know how it is constructed?
- Is the patio going to interfere with the integrity of existing structures?

PLANTING CONSIDERATIONS

If you plan to have a patio with a vine-covered pergola, raised beds and various pockets of planting, you cannot build the patio and then backtrack in order to remove parts of the structure and accommodate these desires – the position of planting areas must be established at design stage.

Decide on planting areas and map them on paper. When you are marking out the patio site on the ground, set out the planting areas and put a frame around them. Make sure that they are kept free of gravel and concrete during the construction process.

FOUNDATIONS

If you are using brick, stone or blocks, you will first need to build a stable foundation under the structure. This will ensure that the structure resists summer and winter ground movement and stays in one piece.

Designing with brick

Good brickwork means designing a structure that minimizes the need to cut bricks; also the vertical joints should be offset in neighboring courses. In most instances, manufactured items such as pre-formed concrete slabs and blocks are compatible with whole brick sizes.

Important principles

Are there any set rules or principles to follow?

The principles that govern the shape of a space, and dictate the character and size of its contents in relation to that space, have gradually evolved over time to produce a set of rules that we know from experience give exciting, well-balanced results, so it is best to adhere to them. Read through the guiding principles described below, and see how they relate to your proposed patio and any other garden structures that are planned.

House and garden

On paper, you might like the idea of symmetry – perhaps a patio centered on the house, with steps centered on the patio – however, you need to consider how this arrangement would affect your use of the patio.

Look at the relationship between the house, garden and patio, decide how you want the elements to come together, and then start thinking about style. Never let form dominate function to the exclusion of everything else.

Doorway into house

Location, orientation, sun, shade and wind

The three most important guiding rules are: location, location, location. Shape, color, texture and design can be changed, but if the location is wrong, everything will feel wrong.

Go into the garden and conduct your own trials. Set out chairs, a table and perhaps an old rug or two, and then over a two- or three-day period, try and get the feel of the location. Is there enough light? Is it a bit drafty? Does the wind whip between the house and a wall to funnel on to the patio? Is there enough dappled shade? If you enjoy sunbathing, can you do it in comfort and sufficient privacy?

Scale and critical measurements

The overall size of the patio, and the size and scale of the units that make it, need to be considered first separately and then together. You might decide that a good size for the patio is 8 yds long and 2 yds wide, but how does this equate to the size of your chosen units? The best plan is to adjust the size of a patio to fit your units. If you plan to use railroad ties, it is much easier to change the size of the patio, rather than cutting the ties.

Drainage slopes

There is nothing quite as miserable as going out on to a patio after a shower and finding water hanging about in puddles and damp spots. Patios must be constructed with a very slight slope in order for water to drain off.

Aesthetics

The dictionary definition of "aesthetics" is "relating to pure beauty rather than any other consideration; artistic or relating to good taste." While it is not easy to decide precisely what is and what isn't good taste, most of us intuitively enjoy some forms and shapes more than others. For example, in patio construction broad curves are usually more acceptable than jagged angles. It is just a matter of fashion whether or not one type of patio surface is thought to be aesthetically pleasing at a particular moment and another is plain vulgar. If you lack confidence, look in books and magazines, ask friends, and draw all this information together to make your designs.

Practicality and feasibility

You might want a patio half the size of the garden, with a partially covered pergola to span it, but you need to balance what is practical against what is feasible. From a practical viewpoint everything might be fine – the levels are right, it doesn't obstruct your view from the house, and your neighbors are happy – but is it feasible? Do you need planning permission? Will the covered pergola make it difficult for you to maintain the house gutters? Will the pergola posts need foundations? Can you afford the cost?

Look at the options, draw up your wish list, assess the costs, and then make a decision.

Sensible layout

Will a large patio impact upon your use of the garden? If the patio is a certain shape and size, will it inhibit access to a gate, or make it difficult to mow the lawn? Will its position block a favorite walk around the garden, or affect the route of paths?

Curves, circles and straight lines

Beautiful sweeping curves excite the senses and draw the eye, but straight lines are easier to build than curved ones. The trick is to get a balance between what you would like, and what is possible on the ground.

For example, the options for creating circles are many and varied: you could buy a circular paver kit, or scribe out a circle and fill it with gravel, bark or concrete. It is not easy to build a circular patio that consists entirely of bricks, because it will involve a lot of cutting; however a brick edging is simple to achieve.

If you want to build a raised patio made from railroad ties, it is best to stay away from circles and curves and go for big, bold, straight lines.

Just as straight lines need to be straight – with no wobbles or curious deviations – so circles and curves need to be just right. Design-wise, broad, sweeping curves are less tense than little tight ones. From a practical viewpoint, it's easier to run the lawnmower around a broad curve than a small one. Curves made from part-circles are the easiest to construct.

Planning and preparation

Now is the time for drawing up lists, working out quantities, scheduling when you are going to do the work, deciding whether or not you need help with the heavier tasks, and phoning around for prices and delivery times. If you put in time at the planning stage working out the fine details – from how much it is going to cost, to where the delivery men are going to put materials, and what happens if it's raining – the project should run in a orderly fashion!

SORTING OUT THE ORDER OF WORK

Each project needs to be planned out according to your particular situation, which is governed by the time of year, the size of your garden, who is helping, and so on. Your initial task is to decide on the order of work – what goes where, and when, and how.

Let's say that you are going to build a large patio of stone pavers. The basic order of work is to dig out the area for the foundation, put down gravel and tamp it flat, spread coarse sand and compact it with a roller or plate compacter, and lay the pavers.

You need to decide in advance where all the excavated earth is going, and where you are going to put the gravel and sand. You don't want them spread out all over the place – you need a clear passage around the garden, and you don't want the materials getting damaged, or posing a safety hazard to children. It's important to plan out each stage and figure out the implications of the procedures in order to avoid unexpected headaches when you start work.

Order for building a paver patio
with stone pavers over sand

Job 6: Finishing
Replace and repair the lawn with turf or grass seed.

Job 5: Joints
Sweep sand into the joints then hose down the patio. Repeat several times with dry sand until joints are full.

Job 4: Frame
Starting with the outer edge, level and gently tamp the pavers in place as you go. Use extra sand below if needed, to ensure each paver is level.

Job 3: Coarse sand
Put at least 2 in of sand over the compacted base, wet it and compact it.

Job 2: Landscape fabric
Adding landscape fabric between the compacted base and the sand is helpful in blocking weeds.

Job 1: Foundation
Dig out the foundation to a depth required by local code and put in compacted gravel, rubble or soil.

Order for building a decorative path
with concrete slabs and rope tile edging

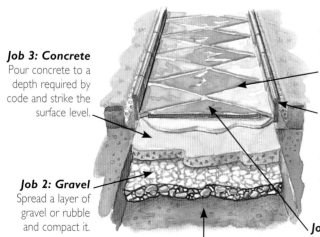

Job 3: Concrete
Pour concrete to a depth required by code and strike the surface level.

Job 2: Gravel
Spread a layer of gravel or rubble and compact it.

Job 1: Foundation
Clear the site, find levels, dig out and compact the base.

Job 6: Finishing
Use a pointing trowel to fill the joints with a dryish mix of mortar.

Job 5: Edging
Bed the rope tile edging in mortar. Pour pea gravel into the gap between the tiles and the earth.

Job 4: Slabs
Bed the slabs on a layer of mortar.

Have you got enough time and energy?

Balance the time available against your energy level. If you are fit, with plenty of time on your hands, you can spread the tasks over weeks instead of days. But if you are short of time, you will need to speed up the procedures. Assuming that you already have good tools, one or more wheelbarrows and plenty of buckets, the biggest single timesaver you can invest in is a cement mixer.

TOOLS AND MATERIALS

Although the choice of materials will depend upon the project, there are two guiding principles: it is always best to use the correct tools for the task, and it is always less expensive to purchase materials in bulk. It may be tempting to use a small garden spade to shift sand rather than buying a new shovel, but it will take you twice as long, and your back will suffer. And don't fall for buying your sand in one pre-packed bag at a time – it will be very expensive!

GETTING QUOTES

You can cut costs by asking for quotes from local companies. List precisely what you want – name of product, size, color and quantity – then phone around for the best price. Never buy materials without seeing them: once you have the quotes, visit the suppliers and look at the products. Having agreed on the price and the delivery date, it is preferable to pay only on delivery of the materials.

HOLIDAYS

Make sure that your schedule takes holidays into account. If you plan to work on a national holiday or a summer weekend, you must order the materials well in advance. You cannot expect companies to deliver at holiday periods or during unsocial hours.

TIMETABLE

If you are short of time, or asking friends to help (or paying for help), you must draw up a timetable. List the procedures and your expectations, and try to stick to completing the tasks in the allotted time. Build in some contingency time in case the weather turns ugly or there are other problems.

Delivery problems

Always assume that deliveries might be late and order your materials well in advance. If you are ordering in bulk, can the delivery truck reach the site? Are you allowed to unload materials on the land in front of your house, or will it pose a hazard? If a crane will be used to winch jumbo bags of sand or pallets of bricks off the truck, is there a convenient spot where they can be lifted over your fence?

CALCULATING MATERIAL QUANTITIES

It is relatively easy to work out how many bricks you need for a particular job (see page 32), but not quite so simple to decide on quantities for sand, cement and gravel. Order sand in bulk, because it is cheaper that way, and if any is left over, use it elsewhere in the garden. Cement is both expensive and short-lived, so order only what you need.

→ *Work out quantities, add on a little extra for good measure, and phone at least three suppliers to ask about prices.*

The shape and size of the brick will dictate how many you need per square yard of path

Plan on a depth of 1 in unless local codes indicate a different depth.

Use pressure-treated wood that is rated for ground contact.

Use rubble or gravel to a depth dictated by local codes.

Work with your local concrete supplier to work out the volume of concrete you'll need.

Landscape fabric for weed block

Guidelines for calculating material quantities

Depending on the project and your local codes, you need to work out the dimensions, the number of pieces (as in bricks) or weight, and then call around to find the best deal.

Gravel ~ Your best deal will come directly from a quarry. If you have a pickup truck or can borrow one from a friend, you can buy a full truckload of gravel at a time. Gravel is sold by weight at the quarry. Typically they weigh your truck as you go in empty and when you leave when full, and charge you for the difference.

Sand ~ Like gravel, sand is sold by weight. And again your best deal will probably be from a local quarry if you have a truck. If not, both gravel and sand can be purchased by the bag, although this can get expensive with a large project.

Concrete ~ Most companies deliver concrete sell by volume, usually in cubic yards. Work with your local supplier to calculate how much you will need. You can also make your own from cement, sand and gravel with a mixer on-site, but this should only be done if you are confident in your abilities or have a friend with experience who can help.

Bricks and blocks ~ Bricks and concrete blocks are usually sold by the pallet-load. Buy a complete load and plan to use the surplus on another project.

WILL YOU NEED SOME HELP?

Building patios can be really good fun. If a friend or relative wants to help, why not agree? You will be giving the helper pleasure and spreading the workload. Digging foundation holes and moving bricks is hard work. Are you fit enough for the tasks ahead? Do you think that you can take a week of bending, lifting, digging and generally slogging it out with buckets and spades? If you have any doubts at all, check with a doctor. The two biggest energy savers are a wheelbarrow and an electric cement mixer, which are worth their weight in gold.

PROTECTING THE SURROUNDING AREA

If you are shifting earth and moving wheelbarrows over the lawn, it's a good idea to protect the grass with a plastic sheet or large sheets of plywood. If you are using a cement mixer, make sure that it is kept well away from the lawn and flowerbeds. Cement is very corrosive: it will damage skin and kill plants, so be careful how you use it. When doing repetitive tasks, such as walking from the cement mixer to the site, or using a wheelbarrow, try to vary the route, to avoid compacting the ground.

Tools and materials

Where do the tools and materials come from?

Tools and materials come from four main sources: DIY stores for tools, builders' merchants for bricks, pavers and tiles, dedicated local suppliers for bulk items such as sand and gravel, and garden centers for fixtures and fittings such as pots, lights and water features. It is possible to make savings – in money by purchasing materials in bulk, in time by using the correct tools for the job, and in effort by buying the best tools that you can afford.

GENERAL CONSTRUCTION TOOLS AND MACHINERY

Tools for measuring and marking

Stakes and string
Small tape measure
Carpenter's level
Big tape measure

Tools for moving materials

Gloves
Wheelbarrow
Bucket

Tools for digging, compacting, mixing and raking

Spade
Shovel
Fork
Sledgehammer
Garden rake
Trowel

Tools for brick, stone, concrete and mortar

Small sledge hammer
Bricklayer's trowel
Mason's hammer
Grinder
Brick chisel
Pointing trowel
Cold chisel

Miscellaneous tools

General-purpose saw
Crosscut saw
Jigsaw
Claw hammer
Rubber mallet
Drill bit (for wood and metal)
Cordless driver
Electric drill
Masonry drill bit (for brick, concrete and stone)
Knife
Flat drill bit (for large holes in wood)
Scissors
Pliers
Metal snips
Screwdriver
Adjustable wrench
Paintbrush

Machinery and power tool safety

Always follow the manufacturer's instructions. Never use electric tools if you are exhausted or taking medication. If the weather is wet or the lawn covered in dew, make sure that you use the tools in conjunction with an electricity circuit breaker. Keep children out of harm's way.

RENTING TOOLS

If you are going to put down a concrete foundation under a structure, you can easily cut time and effort in half by renting a plate compacter to thump the base into place. (This machine is also used for firming paving materials into place.) Mixing mortar and concrete by hand is a chore, but a cement mixer makes the task easy and enjoyable.

GENERAL CONSTRUCTION MATERIALS

Brick and stone

Concrete paver

Artificial stone paver

Real stone paver

Flat stone

Radius paver

Artificial terracotta tile

Imitation stacked tiles (paver)

Building stone

Brick

Artificial stone block

Edging and corner post

Imitation setts

Concrete paving block

Roof tile

Border tile

Slate

Cobbles

Decorative gravel

Wood

Useful timber sections

Rustic post

Log roll

Tie

Log end

Post finial

Trellis

Bark chippings

Fasteners

Zinc-plated wood screw

Zinc-plated metal screw

Galvanized nail

Zinc-plated bolt, washer and nut

Materials for patio water features

Plastic sump pump

Rigid liner

Geo-textile

Butyl liner (thick rubber)

Hose

Armored pipe

Flexible plastic pipe

Flexible copper pipe

KITS

Some small water features are sold in kit form – good if you want an instant effect. At one time, kits comprising reconstituted stone pavers were unconvincing, but now they look almost as good as real stone.

RECLAIMED MATERIALS

Professionally reclaimed materials such as bricks and timber are nearly always a good option in terms of quality and texture, but they can be expensive. If you can, cut costs by doing the reclamation yourself.

CONCRETE AND MORTAR RECIPES

There are as many "best" recipes as there are builders. For successful mixtures, do not use too much water, always use fresh cement and lime, avoid using too much cement in the mortar, and only use clean, well-washed sand.

Cement | Soft sand | Coarse sand | Gravel | Ballast | Lime

Concrete
For foundations (and occasionally pond lining)

For general foundations for block and brick walls

Cement + Coarse sand + Gravel

As above (this recipe uses ballast – a mixture of sand and gravel)

Cement + Ballast

For paths and light-duty foundations

Cement + Ballast

Mortar
For building with bricks, blocks and stone

For bricks and blocks, and general work

Cement + Soft sand

A special soft, smooth mortar for stonework

Cement + Lime + Soft sand

A special rough-textured mortar for wide courses in brick/stonework

Cement + Lime + Coarse sand

CAUTION

Cement and lime powder, wet concrete and mortar are all corrosive!

Wear goggles, a mask and gloves when mixing. If it is a hot or slightly breezy day, you must wash your face after mixing. Wear gloves while building with concrete and mortar.

Setting out the site

I lack confidence – will I be up to the task?

There is only one way to find out if you are equal to the challenge of building a patio, and that is to roll up your sleeves and get started. Measuring, digging, mixing concrete, counting bricks, sawing wood and nailing boards together are all perennial features of the projects, and are within the capabilities of most people. Suppliers are generally happy to offer advice if you are unsure about a process. Make a good start by setting out the site with care.

POINTS TO CONSIDER

- Is your site dry and sandy, hard and rocky, or wet and squashy? You need to dig a trial hole to find out.
- If the ground is very sandy, you must either resite the project or dig much deeper foundations that use a greater thickness of gravel and concrete.
- If the ground is rocky you might not need (or be able) to lay a foundation.
- If the ground is waterlogged, you must either resite the project, or lay pipes underneath the foundations to drain off the excess water.
- If, when you are digging, you come across an unexpected pipe or cable (it might be electricity, water, gas, sewage, oil or land drains), you must stop work and check it out.

CROSS-SECTIONS

A cross-section is a vertical slice through a project, right down to the foundation. Draw a cross-section to help you to visualize how components fit together.

Wall
Patio blocks
Gravel or rubble
Concrete foundation

1. Check your measurements ~ You must measure the thickness of the various materials – for example bricks, mortar courses, foundations – so that you know how deep to dig the hole.

2. Draw to scale ~ Draw cross-sections to scale so that you have a clear understanding of the various layers and the order of work.

MARKING OUT SHAPES

Rectangular shapes

← Hammer in a wooden stake to establish the position of one corner. Tie string to the stake and stretch it taut to set out one side. Turn off at a right angle to set out the next side, and so on until you have four sides marked out with pegs and string. To check the dimensions, measure diagonally from corner to corner and make small adjustments until these measurements are identical – at which time all the corners will be at right angles, if the opposite sides are of equal length.

Circles

← Let's say that you want a circle 6 yds in diameter. Pound a wooden stake into the ground at the point where you imagine the center will be. Cut 3.5 yds of string and tie a loop at each end so that the string is 3 yds long when stretched taut. Slide one loop over the stake and walk around in a circle. When you are happy with the position of the circumference of the circle, slide a long-necked bottle, full of sand, into the other loop and scribe out the circle by pouring the sand out to mark the outer edge.

Curves

← The best way of marking out a free curve is to use a pile of stones and a watering can full of fine, dry sand. Remembering that broad, sweeping curves are easier on the eye than small, tight ones, set out the stones on the ground in what you consider is a good curve. Stand back and see if it looks right. Inspect it from different directions, and live with it for a while.

When you are happy with the curve you have made (and this might take some time), mark the line with a generous trail of sand and remove the stones.

Removing turf

Use a tape measure, stakes and string to mark out the area on the ground. Take a spade and slice up the area into a spade-width grid. Hold the spade at a low angle and slice under the turf to remove one square. Repeat across the whole area.

LEVELS

To create a level area on the ground, start by pounding in a stake at the lowest point. Run a string to the higher ground and pound in another stake. Bridge the two pegs with a length of wood and check with a level. Dig out ground from around the higher stake and along the line of the string until you can reset the second stake lower so that the string and ground below it are level.

DEALING WITH SLOPES

If your ground is sloping, you have three choices. You can bring in materials to build up the slope to make a level plateau; dig into the slope and move the existing soil from the higher point to the lower point to create a level terrace; or give digging and earth-moving a miss, and build a raised decking patio that hovers over the sloping ground.

Much depends on the degree of slope, but for a gently sloping garden, the cheapest option is to define the edge of the patio with a brick retaining wall, and then move the earth within the enclosure until you achieve a level surface.

Earth moved
Move the earth from the higher level to the lower level.

Moved soil retained
Build a wall to retain the moved soil.

Existing ground retained
Dig a trench and build a wall to retain the existing soil.

Drainage
Build weep holes into the base of the walls.

DISPOSING OF EARTH

Digging holes creates waste earth. Topsoil is too precious to throw away and can always be put to good use somewhere in the garden. Subsoil, which is sterile, can be employed at the base of a decorative bank, rock or raised bed, or to fill in a boggy area at the edge of a pond, or banked around the edge of the patio. Try and plan the whole disposal exercise so that the earth only gets moved once, from the hole to its final destination in the garden.

Create a bank around the edge of the patio
To build a bank around the edge of the patio, put the topsoil to one side, dig out the foundations and use the subsoil to create the bank. Allow several weeks for it to settle, and then bring back the topsoil and cover it up.

Fill a dip in the garden
Lay a line of workboards from the foundation hole to the dip in the garden, so that you can run a wheelbarrow full of earth directly to it without damaging the lawn or the path.

Remove from the garden completely
Keep the topsoil. Decide on the shortest possible route from the site to the gate and lay a line of workboards for the wheelbarrow.

BACKHOES

One way to help with excavation is to rent a small backhoe. It will get the task done fast, but will your gates be wide enough? Will a backhoe compact the lawn and scrape the drive? Will it be able to maneuver without damaging borders, trees and other features? If the patio is small, it is probably easier to ask friends to help and dig it by hand. If digging by hand is simply not an option, you have the choice of renting a backhoe and getting down to the task yourself, or renting a backhoe plus driver.

FORMWORK

The sides of a foundation hole need to be stabilized. If the ground is hard, it is not necessary to do anything, but if the ground is soft, you need to use wooden formwork to do this.

Formwork is a frame (like the sides of a shallow box) made from ground contact rated wood. Dig the foundation hole and bang in wooden stakes around the edge, so that they are all at the same level. Screw or nail the formwork boards to them, edge uppermost (the stakes are on the outside of the box).

Foundations

Afoundation is a construction below ground that distributes the weight of a structure so that it is spread over a greater area. It might help to think of the foundation as a raft, and the soil as water – a substance that moves and swells. You can then say that the foundation keeps a structure afloat, in that it stops it from sinking into the soil. The basic rule of making a foundation is the greater the load, the larger the foundation needed.

WHY ARE FOUNDATIONS NEEDED?

Soil is constantly on the move. Depending upon where you live, it swells, slides and heaves when it is wet or frozen, and shrinks, sinks and ripples when it is dry. A foundation acts to spread the load of the structure it supports in such a way that the wall or patio is unaffected by the movement.

The softer the soil and the heavier the structure being built, the larger the foundation needs to be. For small walls in the garden that are no more than 28 in high, a single-brick-thick wall needs a concrete slab that is 4 in thick and twice the width of the wall; while a two-brick-thick wall requires a concrete slab that is 6 in thick and three times the width of the wall.

WHEN ARE THEY NOT NEEDED?

If your site is virgin rock or chalk (meaning that it has never been disturbed), then for small garden structures, such as walls and patios, you can get away without a concrete foundation slab. However, if your site is solid rock and slightly sloping, you will either have to level it out with a wedge-shaped raft of concrete, or build raised decking that floats over the slope (by setting posts in holes full of concrete).

With a foundation

Concrete / Paving slabs

Gravel or rubble

↗ *The weight of the patio and the load it carries are distributed over a wide area. (Walls need deeper, wider foundations.)*

Without a foundation

Soil sinks / Slab slides / Sand shifts

↗ *The subsoil shifts under the weight of the patio, causing it to crack, sink and gradually spread.*

SOIL TYPES AND DRAINAGE

Soil in the average garden usually conforms to these types: sand, clay, heavy loam or a mixture. All soil types have their problems – sand drains well but shifts, clay holds water and is always on the move, and so on. For the most part, you do need to build a foundation, and you have to consider drainage. Dig the foundation area to the required depth. If the earth in the bottom is soft, remove it and replace with a layer of compacted gravel. Lay the concrete slab.

WHAT IF I AM NOT SURE?

If, after digging a few test holes, you are not sure what is going on – maybe the subsoil looks a bit wet and clay-like, and there is a little water in the hole – it is best to go for a generous foundation slab. Dig the foundation hole to a depth required by local code so that you have compacted gravel below a slab of concrete. Ask the advice of a local builder if you are concerned.

QUICK FOUNDATIONS THAT WORK WELL

If test holes reveal that the subsoil is firm, stony and well drained, some structures (such as brick patios and paths) can be built on a foundation of compacted sand over proprietary patio base material. Dig the foundation depth to that specified by local code and set a gravel base, covered with landscaping fabric to prevent weeds growing up through, and then covered with sand before placing the bricks.

LOCAL CONSIDERATIONS

Your choice of sub-base materials will, to a great extent, relate to the local codes enforced in your area. Remember, codes are developed to ensure safety and they do reflect the latest thinking on how to best build quality structures. It cannot be over emphasized that local conditions, even those unique to your small parcel of land on which you are building a patio, may dictate the type of construction you should employ. Check with your local building department.

For safety's sake, always determine if there are electrical power lines, phone lines, or plumbing lines under the area that you are about to push a shovel into. Most local inspection areas will respond within a 48-hour period to mark where lines are so that you can avoid them. Remember that sometimes phone lines are not placed very deep into the ground. The voltage in a phone line is not dangerous, but it is quite the annoyance to be cut off should the line be cut by your digging.

USEFUL FOUNDATIONS

Basic patio and path foundation
for bricks, pavers and small slabs on firm ground

➘ If the foundation hole you have dug is crisp-sided with a dry base, the ground is firm and well drained. If it is a virgin site, compacted paver base over compacted gravel or rubble is generally sufficient, and concrete is not required.

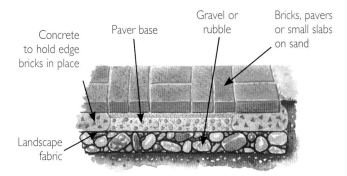

Concrete to hold edge bricks in place · Paver base · Gravel or rubble · Bricks, pavers or small slabs on sand · Landscape fabric

Retained patio or path foundation
for bricks, pavers and small slabs on built-up ground

➘ If the ground has been built up (perhaps a slope has been made from extra earth), the retaining walls need to be two bricks thick, and the foundations for the walls should descend below the level of the built-up ground.

Bricks, pavers or small slabs · Wall and concrete below level of built-up ground · Paver base · Gravel or rubble · Landscape fabric · Original soil level

Extra-solid foundation
for any patio or path on suspect ground

➘ If the ground appears to be soft and spongy, the only safe way to proceed is to assume the worst and go for an extra-deep foundation with good drainage, using gravel and water pipes. On top of this, lay a concrete slab with steel mesh sandwiched in it.

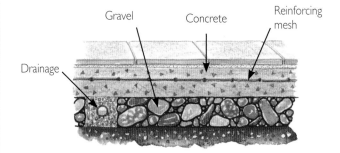

Gravel · Concrete · Reinforcing mesh · Drainage

Simple foundation for a few steps
on firm ground

➘ If the ground is firm and stable, and you want to build a flight of three or four brick and slab steps, a simple foundation of concrete over gravel is adequate.

Concrete slab bedded on mortar · Line of original slope · Firm, well-drained soil · Concrete · Gravel

WHAT KIND OF PATIO FOUNDATION DO I NEED?

Patio type	Type of foundation required
Bricks on firm ground	Dig a foundation depth to match the local code and fill with compacted gravel and an inch-thick layer of sand. Lay the bricks, pour sand into the joints and use a plate compacter to vibrate the patio to a firm, stable finish.
Pavers on an old concrete base	Working on the outer edge of the slab, set a level ring of pavers on a stiff mix of concrete. Cover the slab with coarse sand up to the bottom of the pavers. Set the surface pavers in place, trickle sand into the joints, and use a plate compacter.
Natural bark on wet ground	Dig out the foundation to a depth of 6 in and spread a layer of gravel or shingle, 4 in thick. Cover the gravel with a sheet of landscape fabric. Cover the plastic with 2 in of crushed bark and roll to a smooth finish.
Raised decking on firm ground	Mark the site and location of pressure-treated posts spaced for the maximum allowable joist span. Dig holes per local code, place gravel in the bottom, prop up posts so they are plumb and pour concrete in around the posts.
Pea gravel on firm, uneven ground	Edge the site with formwork: pressure-treated board, fixed to plumb wooden stakes. Spread gravel over the site and pound it to a compacted finish. Fill the formwork with well-washed pea gravel.

Problems with the site

What do I do if I have problems?

If you have considered, planned and designed the project as described in previous pages, any problems that crop up should only be small ones – just tiny details that you have overlooked. These last-minute hitches are easily rectified, simply by standing back and taking a fresh look at the situation, and then making small alterations. Some sites and situations are potentially more problematic, however; ways to head off trouble are described below.

SMALL SPACES

If you would like to create a patio in a small space, for example a narrow garden about 3 yds wide with high walls all around, it is best not to try and squeeze a small patio into a small garden, but rather to turn the whole garden into one large patio.

LOOKING UPWARDS

If you cannot spread outwards, how about upwards? Hang or grow plants on walls, disguising the boundaries of the area and giving the impression that there is more space.

DARK SPACES

With the right concealed lighting, a small, dark, unexciting space can become a place of mystery and promise. Turn it into a shrine, secret place, cavern or retreat.

By building upwards, this seaside home cleverly fits two complementary patios into the garden without losing any extra space. The raised patio is a haven for sunbathing and enjoying the view, and the lower patio provides a shady escape from the sun.

A WINDY, EXPOSED SITE

A site may have a wonderful view, but be at the mercy of the wind. You have four options: build elsewhere, plant a fast-growing hedge, build a sunken patio with a bank around it, so that the wind whips over your head, or, best of all (if you have the money) build a feature wall on the exposed side.

SLOPING SITES

If a site has a gentle slope, you can build a retaining wall and level the site with gravel. If the slope is extreme, the most exciting option is to build a raised decking patio that straddles the slope like a seaside pier.

ALMOST RIGHT, BUT NOT QUITE

The 'almost-right-but-not-quite' scenario can only be solved with the passing of time. If you know something is not right, but cannot quite put your finger on the problem, it is best to live with the patio for a while and hope that over time, you will gradually be able to assess faults and put them right.

SURPLUS OF READY-MIXED CONCRETE

If you have ordered too much ready-mixed concrete, there are three sensible options. You can swiftly dig out a foundation for a new construction – a path or shed – and cast a concrete slab, or you can donate it to a neighbor. The most unappealing option is to cast it into small, portable blobs and take these to the dump.

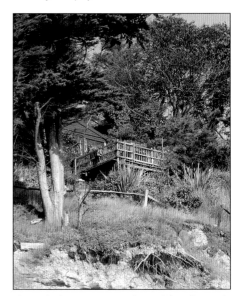

An artist's retreat complete with a dramatic raised decking patio built to take advantage of a spectacular view over an estuary. Raised decking easily copes with problems caused by a steeply sloping site such as this.

CONSULT THE PATIO SITE DOCTOR

Digging a hole is not always as straightforward as you might imagine. The exciting thing about pushing a spade into the ground is the unpredictability of what it will reveal. Of all the problems involved with building patios, those associated with digging the foundations are the most common. One moment you are digging a hole, and the next moment something happens and a problem rears its ugly head. Don't go into a dizzy panic, but stand back and look at the problem, list possible solutions and then act accordingly. If the worst comes to the worst and the problem seems totally insurmountable, get professional advice.

If possible, try to avoid problems by looking at site plans and checking for drains, water pumps, wells, gas lines and power cables before you finally settle on a location.

Problem	*Solution*
You are digging a hole, you chop through something hard, the hole fills with black, foul-smelling water.	If the water is black, the likelihood is that you have chopped through a landscape drainage pipe. Wait until the water stops rising, and then use a bucket to bale out the hole. If you see a damaged pottery drain, bridge the hole with a sheet of tin and cover it with concrete.
You are digging a hole and you discover a massive tree root just below the surface of the ground.	Being very careful not to damage the root, ring it (giving it a wide berth) with a mini brick wall and fill the central area with earth topped with gravel. The wall and gravel will become an attractive feature, rather like a piece of sculpture.
You are digging a hole and discover concrete foundations just below the surface of the ground.	You can save time and money by incorporating the old foundations into the new. If the foundations are totally unexpected and look very old, perhaps even ancient, make contact with a local history society before you proceed.
You are digging a hole and chop through a water main – there is fresh water gushing out.	You need to turn off the main water. Go out into the road, just by the front gate but still on your property, and look for a small lid that conceals the main supply valve. Lift the lid and turn off the valve. In cold climates, your main supply valve may be inside your basement. Phone the emergency number for the water company immediately.
You are digging a hole and come across a trench lined and bridged with slabs of stone.	The chances are that you have struck an old soakaway trench from a garden septic tank or cesspool, or, if your house is old, from your kitchen sink waste pipe, or even from a local spring. Don't disturb it, simply build over or around it.
You are digging a hole and discover a pit full of builders' rubble.	If the rubble is compacted and full of earth, build the foundation over it. If there is a sheet of rusted corrugated iron over the pit, the pit is a rainwater soakaway. Replace the corrugated iron with new, cover it with a slab of concrete and continue work.
You are digging a hole and find a brick well, covered with a stone slab, with water in the bottom.	Wonderful – what a find! Remove the stone slab and lay new bricks on the old to bring the sides of the well above what will be the surface of the patio. When the patio is finished, trim the well with a lid and winding handle and make a feature of it.
You are digging a hole and discover ancient pottery, old coins and a human skull.	Really exciting – what and who have you found? Stop work immediately and report your find first to the police and then to the local archaeological society. Don't carry on digging, don't try to polish up the coins, and don't touch the skull – wait until they have been assessed by professionals.
You are digging a hole and come across a huge boulder as big as a giant pumpkin.	Remove the earth until all the sides of the rock are revealed, and then little by little, with an iron bar and wedges, lever it out of the hole. When the patio is finished, bring the rock back on site and make it into a feature, as might be used in a Japanese garden.
You are digging a hole and fine sand pours out of the sides of the hole.	The sand indicates that the subsoil is unstable and not suitable for digging holes. It is best to build a raft of concrete on the ground. Pour a concrete slab with a thickness determined by local code and that contains rebar.

Patio shapes and styles

Patios have come a long way since the grim old days when the best you could hope for was eight concrete paving slabs and a couple of beach chairs. Today you can have a patio in just about any shape, style and size that you like. A patio is now required to be more than just a dry, level area – it is a garden room where you can relax, have a barbecue, spend time with family and friends, and enjoy a view of the garden for many months of the year.

PATIO SHAPES

Plan the shape of the patio to suit your needs. What is the patio going to be used for? Do you want it to relate to the shape of the garden? Do you want it to reflect the character of the house? Do you have strong preferences for certain materials? How much money do you want to spend? Your answers to these questions will, to a great extent, decide the shape and character of the patio that you build.

Basic rectangular

↗ *A modest rectangular patio set close to (and square with) the house. It is level with the lawn and a good option for a small garden.*

Rectangular combinations

↗ *An L-shaped patio, made from two linked rectangles, level with the lawn. It is designed to fit around existing features.*

Circular (also hexagonal, octagonal)

↗ *Strong shapes – such as circles and hexagons – are attractive and decorative. They make beautiful island patios in a large sea of lawn, trees, shrubs and flower borders.*

Geometrical combinations

↗ *Geometrical combinations, for example circles joined to rectangles, or linked circles, are not only wonderfully dynamic in their own right, but can be used to create small patio "rooms."*

Organic

↗ *An informal, flowing shape can look perfect in a large wild garden, making a natural sitting area that is like a clearing.*

Complex

↗ *Complex forms are good when you need to create a number of small areas at different levels to suit a steeply sloping site.*

Split levels and shape

Linked shapes allow you to create split-level areas. So, for example, you might have a circle linked to a rectangle, with the rectangle forming the main "room" of the patio, and the circle making a smaller "room" slightly raised to one side. This linked split-level two-room design, with one room approached by a small flight of steps, creates a private area, like an intimate den. (See page 38.)

PATIO STYLES

Just like castles, houses, bungalows and cottages, patios can be designed to relate to a regional or historical style. If you enjoy all things French, Mediterranean or Swiss, delight in English seaside style, or have a passion for Victoriana or the American Wild West, there's no reason at all why your patio cannot use that style as a reference point.

↗ *A porch decking patio with a Mediterranean feel. Angular raised beds made of bleached wood host a minimalistic planting scheme. Azure gravel surrounds the plants, providing a practical mulch, but also echoing the shimmering colors of sea and sky.*
↖ *A traditional patio in the Old English cottage style, given a modern twist by the addition of contemporary furniture. The patio is slightly raised to cope with a sloping site.*

PATIO STYLES AND THEMES

STYLE / THEME	TYPICAL MATERIALS / COMPONENTS
Old English Cottage A style that was popular in England and America in the 1930s.	*Lots of red brick and tile surfaces, columns, pergolas, stone ball finials and formal fishponds. A high standard of bricklaying expertise, with central steps running down to a lawn. Vegetable garden and lots of roses.*
American Wild West Images familiar from American cowboy films.	*Lots of decking: a board patio hard against the house, covered with a porch and surrounded with balustrades made up of distressed boards. Wooden steps, water barrel, gingerbread trim, picket fences and lots of white paint. Simple flower borders.*
Japanese Garden A calm, ordered look inspired by nature and the tea ceremony.	*An area of flagstones, with a wooden walkway running across a stream. Large feature rocks, collections of stones, cobbles, and raked sand or gravel. Ferns, moss, stone water bowls and troughs, willow, bamboo and bonsai trees.*
English Seaside A jolly design framework from the seaside culture of the 1950s.	*An area of raised decking with a narrow wooden pier or walkway and a cobble and sand beach. Deckchairs, striped canvas awning, fairy lights strung between posts, benches with cast-iron ends. Grasses, driftwood and glass fishing floats.*
Mediterranean Hotel Whitewashed walls, bright flowers; a snapshot of a sun-drenched retreat.	*A level, paved area with rendered and white-painted block walls to the sides. Raised pools, café chairs and tables, bleached wood benches. Simple, clean lines, modern lighting. Gravel, colored tiles, raised beds with drought-tolerant planting.*
Old Spanish Courtyard Stylish and intricate North African references: mysterious and striking.	*A private courtyard area with high walls to the sides and a low, formal pond at the center. Lots of symmetry and surfaces decorated with ceramic mosaics in geometrical patterns, circles, triangles and zigzags. A Moorish arch feature.*

Quick patios

Is it possible to build a patio in a weekend?

Much depends upon your skills and motivation, and how many friends you can rope in to help, but if you spend a week or so making plans and preparing the ground, there is no reason at all why you cannot complete a patio in a long weekend. It would be hard work, and mean starting the project last thing on the Friday, and continuing through Saturday and Sunday, but by the Monday you could be lying flat out on the patio!

QUICK GRAVEL PATIO

If your site is more or less level, gravel is an easy option.

Start by removing the turf and digging down about 4 in. Pile the topsoil round the sides and use a spade and rake to sculpt it into a long, low mound. Edge the excavated area with wooden boards, so that they stand clear by about 1 in.

Fill the recess to within an inch of the top of the board with compacted gravel and top it with washed pea gravel. Turf the mound. Furnish the patio with a picnic table, benches, deckchairs and a barbecue. Arrange pot plants around the sides.

Step 2
Pile the soil around the sides and shape it into a long, low mound.

Step 3
Pound in stakes at corners and at regular intervals around the excavation. Fix the boards in place.

Step 4
Put a layer of compacted gravel into the recess. Top with pea gravel.

Step 5
Add landscape fabric on top of the gravel.

Step 1
Use stakes and string to mark out the site. Remove the turf and topsoil.

Step 6
Turf the mound, arrange pot plants and furnish the patio.

QUICK DECKING PATIO

Decide on the size of the patio and divide it up into a 1 yd grid, like a checkerboard. Clear the turf away from the site.

Dig holes at the corners and grid intersections. Half-fill the holes with hardcore. Cover the site with landscape fabric. Dig footings according to local codes and set precast concrete piers on top of the footings.

Use treated wood to build a framework. Sit the framework on the concrete blocks. Cover the frame with decking boards screwed with rust-resistant screws to the framework.

Step 2
Use precast concrete piers bedded on top of the footing in concrete.

Step 3
Cover the site with sheets of landscape fabric covered with an inch of loose gravel.

Step 4
Build the frame from either pressure-treated wood rated for ground contact or rot-resistant wood.

Step 1
Mark out the grid, clear away the turf and dig holes to the depth required by local code and fill with gravel and then concrete.

Another decking idea

To build decking that is raised off the ground, cut posts to the same level and use concrete to fix them in the holes.

QUICK FOUNDATIONS FOR PAVED PATIOS

There are two swift ways of laying patio slabs: on a stiff mix of concrete, or on compacted sand. Both require a similar foundation and preparation.

Mark out the site and clear the turf and topsoil down to the depth required by code. Pound stakes in to mark the height of the base and make sure the stakes are level with each other. Compact gravel or rubble in the bottom and then use sand or concrete depending on if you are using method 1 or 2.

➜ *Prepare the site by digging to the depth required by local code. Lay a base of compacted gravel and the cover with compacted sand to the height of the stakes.*

Method 1
Slabs on compacted sand

Stakes pounded into the ground to mark the height of the base

Paving slabs set on compacted sand and gravel below

Dig deep enough to meet local codes

Compacted gravel or rubble

Landscape fabric to block weeds

Method 2
Slabs on concrete

Stakes pounded into the ground to mark the height of the base

Paving slabs set directly on moist concrete

Excavate to depth required by local code

Compacted gravel or rubble

➜ *Prepare the site by compacting gravel or rubble to the depth required by code. Spread a dryish, stiff mix of concrete to the level of the top of the stakes. Carefully position the slabs directly on the moist concrete.*

Wet or clay ground

If the ground consists of clay or is wet, dig out the foundation to the depth required by code and use metal fencing or rebar in the concrete for reinforcement. Allow the concrete to set and place the slabs in fresh mortar on top of the concrete.

GOOD DESIGN CAN SAVE YOU EFFORT

Rectangular shapes are much easier to build than circles or hexagons. Design the patio so that it uses a number of whole units – bricks, concrete slabs, pavers, decking boards or whatever. If the site is sloping, avoid heavy digging and concrete mixing by going for raised decking. As far as possible, design the patio so that it uses local materials, because this will cut effort and costs.

GOOD PLANNING CAN SAVE YOU TIME

Order all the materials weeks beforehand. Plan the project so that you can complete it in good weather. Clear and prepare the site well in advance of the actual building work. Cover the area immediately around the site with workboards and tarpaulins, so that you don't do irreparable damage to the lawn. Make sure that you have all the tools that you need. Plan the work in day-length chunks.

GETTING EXTRA HELP

Canvass help from family and friends well in advance, so that they can plan their time accordingly. If the task is really daunting, get a contractor to do some of the heavy work, such as digging the foundations and compacting the hardcore. If you are asking friends to help, make sure that they have the correct tools for the job. Make sure that all your workers have protective gloves.

USING MACHINES TO SPEED UP THE WORK

Renting a machine might seem to be an extra cost, but it can save money by cutting down your work time. An electric concrete mixer is a boon for mixing concrete. A power-driven plate compacter is great when you have to compact a lot of gravel. If you are building wooden decking, an electric miter saw (chop saw) and one or more battery-driven screwdrivers will save you hours of hard work.

IS YOUR QUICK PATIO SAFE TO USE?

A patio must be safe, with no slippery slabs, badly built steps, or uneven paving slabs waiting to trip you up. If you have any doubts at all about the suitability of materials or the size of fixings required, seek professional advice. Most builders' merchants are happy to give guidance.

MORE QUICK PATIOS

Soft sand ~ A large area of soft sand makes a good patio for a family with toddlers – it is easy to build, safe and fun to use. You just dig out a shallow hole and fill it with clean sand.

Crushed bark ~ Crushed bark is wonderful for a natural patio with a forest-glade effect – it is firm and dry underfoot, easy to build, economical, safe for children and eco-friendly.

Decking boards ~ Decking squares set in pea gravel make a fast, easy patio. Great for a temporary patio.

Basic patios

If you enjoy simple garden structures that are solidly built and will last a lifetime, a basic no-frills rectangular patio is an appropriate choice. There are three good options: a patio made from concrete paving slabs, a decking patio made from off-the-shelf decking boards (will suit a small, modern garden), and a patio made from kiln-fired clay bricks (excellent for creating a traditional-looking patio suitable for the garden of a cottage or townhouse).

HOW TO BUILD A BASIC PATIO OUT OF CONCRETE PAVERS

Several shapes of reconstituted stone slab, which look convincingly like the real thing, have been used for this patio.

Choose your slab type, measure its size, and decide how big you want the patio to be (in whole slabs).

Use stakes and string to mark the area on the ground. Remove the turf and topsoil to the depth required by code. Take a number of wooden stakes and hammer them (at 1 yd intervals over the site) into the ground so that they are level and stand proud so that their tops will be the height of the bottom of your slabs.

Cover the site with compacted gravel topped by compacted coarse sand. Finally, ease the slabs into place and fill the joints between them with sand.

Step 5
Place landscape fabric on the compacted gravel and cover with compacted sand to the level of just above the top of the stakes.

Step 6
Set the slabs in place. Brush sand into the joints between them.

Step 1
Mark out the site with stakes and string, so that the patio is made up of a number of whole slabs. You might need to work around obstructions.

Step 4
Compact gravel to make the base and cover with landscape fabric.

Step 3
At 1 yd intervals, pound in more stakes to stand level with the first.

Step 2
Excavate to a depth required by local code. Pound a stake into the ground until its top is at the intended height of the bottom of the slabs.

HOW TO BUILD A BASIC PATIO OUT OF DECKING

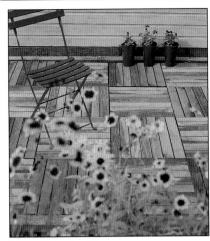

This simple patio made of decking tiles adjoins a seaside cabin. Slight variations in shade between the tiles add interest.

➜ Raised decking is a good option for sloping ground, or where you have to work over things such as drains and old foundations. Use 4x4 in square section for the posts. The size and spacing of beams, joists and decking depend on the type of wood used and local codes. Consult your local building department.

Step 4
Divide up the beams with joists nailed to the beams and posts. Space joists according to code.

Step 5
Nail spacers between the joists to stop them twisting.

Step 6
Finally, cover the whole frame with decking boards nailed to both beams and joists. Leave a ⅛ in gap between each board.

Step 1
Mark out the site and dig holes to the depth advised by local code. Put gravel in the bottom.

Step 2
Set all the posts squarely into the holes and make sure that they are level. Fill the holes with concrete.

Step 3
Bolt the outer ring of beams to the posts. Cut off the posts level with the beams.

HOW TO BUILD A BASIC PATIO OUT OF BRICKS

←↘ A brick patio is expensive; however it is easy to build, attractive, and will last a lifetime. Mark out the site and remove the turf and topsoil. Ring the site with a mini brick wall, then fill the central area with compacted gravel topped with compacted coarse sand and raked soft sand. Lay the bricks in position and fill the joints with sand. Finally, use a plate compacter to settle the bricks into place.

A traditional patio made from high-fired bricks. The herringbone design – with the bricks set square to the sides – keeps brick-cutting to a minimum.

Step 4
Set the pattern of bricks in place. Fill the joints with sand. Use a plate compacter to consolidate the bricks.

Step 3
Cover the gravel with compacted coarse sand up to the level of the pegs.

Step 1
Remove turf and topsoil down to the depth required by code, place stakes throughout to mark the height of the bottom of the bricks and lay a base of compacted gravel.

Step 2
Spread a layer of concrete around what will be the perimeter of the patio, and set the edge bricks in place so that they are level with each other.

Real stone patios

Are patios made of real stone difficult to build?

Real quarried stone is more expensive than reconstituted stone (a mixture of crushed stone and concrete), but its beauty as a material is hard to match. To build a patio from it involves a lot of hard work moving heavy slabs of stone. Once a real stone patio is in place, it transcends fads and fashions and will last a lifetime. This type of patio will slot equally well into a traditional or modern garden, with the ability to blend into any decorative scheme.

To save money, this patio has been made from salvaged stone. Instead of obscuring the attractive stone surface with lots of containers, plants tumble from hanging baskets.

ADVANTAGES AND DISADVANTAGES

Advantages of real stone

✔ Looks good in its own right and doesn't need to be treated or painted.

✔ Lasts a lifetime.

✔ The color doesn't fade and just looks better with the passing years.

✔ It makes very attractive crazy paving – a design solution that is perfect for those who enjoy attention to detail.

Disadvantages of real stone

✘ Real stone slabs are expensive.

✘ Delivery and handling costs are high.

✘ It must be laid on a solid foundation of compacted gravel and concrete, and pointed with mortar.

✘ Real stone slabs are very heavy – you need to be strong and fit, and you might need help with the lifting.

OPTIONS FOR REAL STONE PATIOS

Real stone pavers

Though pavers made from real cut stone are both expensive and difficult to source, they are an exciting option.

Reclaimed stone with gravel gaps

Reclaimed flagstones, set together for best fit, with the joints between them filled with pea gravel and planted with herbs.

Crazy paving

Crazy paving is a good choice if you want a relatively cheap patio. The stone is bedded on blobs of mortar.

Setts

Setts come in many types and sizes. Salvaged setts from city roads may be available from local sources.

Decorative combinations

Brick and stone look really good together – perfect if you want to create a low-cost patio for your garden.

Random, worn-top field stones, set together for best fit, with the wide courses planted with grass and wildflowers.

Real stone tips

The secret of working with stone is to do your best to use the pieces as you find them, and keep cutting to a minimum. Salvaged stone, which could be described as stone that has been worked by someone else, is good from this point of view. It varies in thickness, so needs to be set on generous blobs of mortar.

FOUNDATIONS

To provide a firm footing for a real stone patio, the foundation should be as deep as required by code. Variations of soil type and weather conditions make depth a local consideration. Each slab is set on mortar (one blob at each corner and in the center); joints are filled with mortar.

TYPES OF REAL STONE

Slate
Gray to brown, smooth and shiny. Breaks easily into flat pieces.

Sandstone
Gold through to green, with a sandy texture. Breaks into flat pieces.

Limestone
White and soft. Reclaimed stone is good for walls and edge detailing.

Granite
Gray to green, with some sparkly bits. Reclaimed setts are very attractive.

When you go to look at real stone at a builders' merchant or reclamation yard, you will be presented with lots of types, such as "York stone" or "Pennsylvania stone." Don't worry about the names, other than to find out whether the stone is slate, sandstone, limestone or granite. If the stone is hard, a pleasant color and presents at least one flat face, it is suitable for use in a patio. Slate is good because it splits naturally into thin, flat pieces and is a good color. Sandstone splits well, is an appealing color, and has a very attractive sandy texture. Limestone works well as small pieces for walls and steps, but looks a bit slick as large slabs. Granite setts are perfect for patios and paths.

HOW TO LAY REAL STONE SLABS

⤵ Dig out the earth where the patio will be situated to the depth required by the local code. Level the site. Set each slab on a dryish mix of concrete (concrete that has been mixed with the minimum of water). Level the slabs with each other. Use a trowel to fill the joints with mortar. For another construction method with an even more solid foundation, see the "Foundations" box on page 26.

Step 1
Use a tape measure, stakes and string to set out the area on the ground. Dig out the earth and level the area.

Step 2
Put down boards to make formwork (defines the patio's shape and contains the foundation).

Step 3
Concentrating on one slab at a time, put down a shovelful of concrete and set the slab in place and adjust the level.

Step 4
When the concrete under the slabs is dry, use a small pointing trowel to fill the joints with a dryish mix of mortar.

HOW TO BUILD A CRAZY-PAVING PATIO

Try to arrange the stones so that the gaps are a similar width

Fill (point) the gaps with mortar

Build a foundation using 200 mm of compacted gravel topped with coarse sand. Practice arranging a small area to see how the pieces of stone will fit together best. Although you can cut or break stone to fit (see page 71), keep cutting to a minimum. Use big pieces in the middle and smaller pieces towards the outside. Set the stones on a generous layer of a dryish mix of concrete. Point the gaps with mortar. (See page 39 for how to build a circular crazy-paving patio.)

HOW TO BUILD A PATIO USING SETTS

Reclaimed granite sett

Dry-mix mortar brushed into joints

Generous amount of mortar

Compacted gravel topped with a skim of sand

Fill the foundation with gravel and cover with sand. One sett at a time, spread a layer of mortar over the sand and press the sett into the mortar. Aim for the mortar to be about an inch lower than the top of the setts. Brush dry-mix mortar into the joints.

USEFUL TIPS

• Be generous with the gravel and make sure it is well compacted.
• Use coarse sand, not soft (or builder's) and make sure it is well compacted.
• For large areas, it's worth renting a plate compacter machine to vibrate the gravel and sand into place.
• If you can't afford real stone, consider using reconstituted stone. Some of the modern products are good enough to fool the eye into believing that they are the genuine article.

Reconstituted stone patios

Is reconstituted stone as good as real stone?

Reconstituted stone consists of concrete plus an aggregate of ground-up stone. At one time, reconstituted stone was rather unattractive, with a uniform texture and only available in a selection of harsh colors. However, modern reconstituted stone is so convincing that it is almost impossible to tell it apart from the genuine article. Stone pavers are particularly good – colors, cast patterns and textures vary from slab to slab to give a realistic effect.

ADVANTAGES AND DISADVANTAGES

Advantages of reconstituted stone

✔ Readily available in lots of grades, textures, colors and sizes.

✔ It is many times less expensive than real stone – a fraction of the cost.

✔ Because it is a uniform size and thickness, it is perfect for a patio.

✔ It doesn't have a grain so it is less likely to be damaged by extremes in temperature.

Disadvantages of reconstituted stone

✘ The colors of some low-grade types can fade over time – sometimes in just a couple of years.

✘ It doesn't have the subtle texture of real stone – there are no sparkly bits on sides and edges.

✘ It doesn't age as well as real stone, and doesn't develop a delicate patina and textural subtlety.

FOUNDATIONS

Just like real stone, reconstituted stone needs a good, solid foundation. (See page 16 for more about foundations.)

A medium-sized patio made from reconstituted stone slabs. Note the subtle textures and the way the random design is made up from a number of modules consisting of different slabs – a large square, a quarter-square and a rectangle.

HOW TO LAY RECONSTITUTED STONE SLABS ON FIRM GROUND

↘ Dig the patio foundation: remove the earth to the depth required by the local code. Level the site. Set each slab on a dryish mix of concrete (concrete that has been mixed with the minimum of water). Level the slabs with each other. Use a trowel to fill the joints with mortar. For another construction method with an even more solid foundation, see the "Foundations" box on page 26.

Step 5
When the concrete has set, use a small trowel to tool mortar into the joints. Finally, when the mortar has partly set, use a brush to clean the joints.

Step 4
Standing on a plank or workboard, carefully set the pavers in place. Level and adjust each slab as you go.

Step 3
Working from one side to another, spread a dryish mix of concrete over the whole site. Level and tamp the concrete with a long board.

Step 1
Use a tape measure, stakes and string to set out the area on the ground. Dig out the earth to the depth required by the local code.

Step 2
Edge the excavation with boards, staked and nailed into place.

OPTIONS FOR RECONSTITUTED STONE PATIOS

Colors and textures

Weathered stone is a silver-gray color and looks almost black when it is wet.

Old-style stone – light gray with a touch of green – turns a rich slate gray when it is wet.

Weathered red stone (reddish stone with pools of brick red) looks almost red when wet.

Weathered buff – a hot creamy yellow – ages to a gentle, paler cream.

Other paving components

Slabs that mimic old, weathered bricks are very good for edgings and small details to break up large areas of plain paving.

Blocks designed to look like stone setts.

Walling blocks can be used to edge a patio (especially effective around raised decking and to edge small, formal ponds).

Slabs designed to look like old terracotta tiles are ideal for small details, edges and steps, when you want to inject some color.

Kits

This octagonal kit, with an octagon at the center, makes a wonderful detail set within a large, formal patio made up of square and rectangular slabs.

A radius kit used to circle a small, round patio and form an overall square shape. Gravel and plants frame the shape and give added visual emphasis.

CUTTING PAVERS

First, cut a groove across the slab.

It is best to cut reconstituted stone pavers with an electric angle grinder. You will also need a brick chisel and a small sledge hammer. Start by marking the line of cut with chalk. Wearing protective goggles, a dust mask and gloves, use the grinder to cut a groove, 2–3 mm deep, across the slab. Cut the groove slightly deeper at the corners.

Sit the slab on the grass. Now, with a brick chisel in one hand and a small sledge hammer in the other, set the chisel on the groove and give it a series of light taps with the small sledge hammer. If you are doing it correctly, you will hear the sound gradually change, until suddenly the slab falls into two pieces. Don't rush the process, and don't be tempted to give the slab a single blow.

Use a brick chisel to break the slab.

Useful tips

Take your time choosing materials and putting down a foundation, and you won't be disappointed with the patio that results.

Kit cost ~ Kits come in many sizes, types, textures and colors. Make sure you get one with a guarantee. Kits are a good option for a very small patio, but do work out quite expensive for anything wider than about 2 yds.

Kit quality ~ Never buy a "bargain" kit – the slabs will probably be very thin and made from a very weak mix of concrete. Test for cracks by rapping the slabs with your knuckles. A sound slab will give a tuneful ring like a bell.

Window dressing ~ Consider buying top-quality plain slabs, and make them special by trimming with a feature such as a special brick edging or a mini wall.

Efflorescence (white stain) ~ Thin white stains (a sort of powdery coating) are normal. They will gradually vanish of their own accord. If you wish, efflorescence can be removed with a special wash and the patio then protected with masonry sealant.

Natural patios

Are natural patios difficult to create?

A natural patio appears to be an easy option, because it is no more than a little haven built using natural materials to imitate nature, decorated with lots of planting. However, this appearance of simplicity is not easy to achieve. The best way to proceed is to find a perfect glade or dell, then do your best to copy its shape and form, and the way it is positioned in relation to the sun. Leave it to time and nature to do the rest, gradually blending it into the landscape.

WHAT ARE NATURAL PATIOS?

A natural patio is a resting place – a sheltered, warm, sunny spot, perhaps with just the right amount of dappled shade; a cosy, dry place that invites you to stop, look and linger. It could reproduce the sort of area that walkers might seek out to take a break, or represent your favorite type of scenery or beauty spot.

For some, the perfect place might be a gravel-covered area by a beach, with rocks and patches of low planting; for others, the ideal retreat would be a forest glade, with a leaf-mold floor, a fallen tree, trees and bushes dotted about, and a sea of bluebells. An old-fashioned meadow, crammed with cornflowers, poppies and tall grasses waving in a gentle breeze, with a mown area to hide in, might also appeal.

➜ *An area of lawn set within a copse, and designed to look like a natural forest glade, makes a perfect retreat. This patio is cheap to make, so you can afford to spend more on a good quality garden seat.*

NATURAL PATIO OPTIONS

Orchard clearing

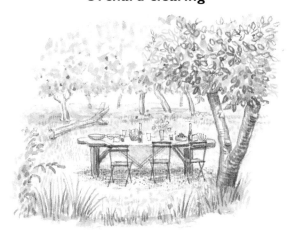

↗ This perfect natural patio takes advantage of a beautiful orchard with fruit trees and lush meadow grass. The area forming the patio has been levelled with a thick layer of gravel for drainage, and topped with a layer of wood chips or bark. The huge table (made from a slab of wood) is a permanent feature, and is great for informal meals. The fallen tree is a favorite play area for children.

Pond-side retreat

➜ Patios and ponds make the perfect partners – great if you enjoy watching all the wildlife associated with a pond. The area is defined by large rocks and covered by gravel topped with pea gravel. The gravel ensures that there is a dry, level area, which allows you to spread a blanket, have a sumptuous picnic, and then stretch out and relax.

Forest hideaway

➜ Robinson Crusoe might have enjoyed this natural patio in a forest clearing, surrounded by trees. The hut blends into the leaf-covered forest floor to make a wonderful hideaway.

HOW TO CREATE A PATIO IN A MATURE ORCHARD

Wait for a warm summer's day, then take a chair into the orchard and sit in what you consider is a good spot. Observe how the sun moves in relation to the trees and existing buildings, and generally look at the area with a view to sitting there with family and friends for an informal meal.

Stake out the area that you want to be level and drained, bearing in mind that people tend to take up more space when they are out of doors. Remove the turf and topsoil and spread a generous layer of compacted and rolled gravel, followed by a sheet of landscape fabric. Top with crushed bark. For a truly natural look, use tree stumps for tables and seating.

Existing fruit trees
Trees cut back, trimmed and pruned, so that they set the scene. Old trees could be sculpted to provide additional seating.

Wooden bench
Old wooden benches always come in useful and look good, blending into the scene with ease.

Crushed bark
Crushed bark provides the perfect natural surface – it is firm and dry underfoot, safe for children to play on, and biodegradable.

Drained and levelled
Turf and topsoil removed. Layer of compacted and rolled gravel laid and levelled, and covered with landscape fabric. Topped with a thick layer of crushed bark.

Tree stumps
Well-placed tree trunks provide seating for children, while sawn sections provide informal tables and seats for adults.

HOW TO MAKE A SEASIDE-THEMED PATIO

Choose a spot that is dry and exposed, and gets as much sunshine as possible. Remove the turf and topsoil, and level the area with rolled gravel. Cover the gravel with fine crushed rock or shingle.

Buy as many rocks as you can afford (preferably flat with weathered edges and a water-washed appearance). Lay the rocks with generous gaps around them, and fill these with pebbles and sand. Plant a selection of seaside flowers such as sea lavender and thrift. Dress the area with seaside finds such as driftwood, lengths of rope, shells or even an old rowing boat.

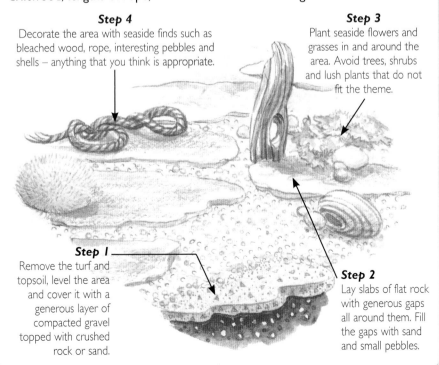

Step 4
Decorate the area with seaside finds such as bleached wood, rope, interesting pebbles and shells – anything that you think is appropriate.

Step 3
Plant seaside flowers and grasses in and around the area. Avoid trees, shrubs and lush plants that do not fit the theme.

Step 1
Remove the turf and topsoil, level the area and cover it with a generous layer of compacted gravel topped with crushed rock or sand.

Step 2
Lay slabs of flat rock with generous gaps all around them. Fill the gaps with sand and small pebbles.

HOW TO CREATE A MEADOW CLEARING

Choose a level spot in an existing lawn and mow a sitting area. Let the surrounding grass grow tall. Plant selected areas with as many species of meadow flowers as you can find. Keep the area clear of nettles and brambles.

Themes and props

A themed natural patio needs to be dressed with the appropriate props, rather like a film set. Bales of hay and old farm machinery will enhance a meadow; tree stumps and sawing horses will make a forest glade look authentic; rocks, shale and alpine plants will suit a mountain dell.

Brick or paver patios

Does it take a long time to lay a brick patio?

If you enjoy geometrical patterns, a brick patio is a good project to choose. Because bricks are fairly small, they do take longer to lay than paving slabs, for example. However, working with bricks is a wonderfully therapeutic activity, and there is something really satisfying about the way they fit together. Bricks have six sides: two end or "header" faces, two side or "stretcher" faces, a top or "frog" face and a bottom face. The pattern bricks are laid in is termed the bond.

TYPES OF CLAY BRICK

Bricks come in hundreds of colors and textures, with an actual size of 3 ⅝ x 2 ¼ x 8 in when calculating quantities for a project, ½ in-thick mortar joints are allowed for. For patios, use well-fired (or high-fired) exterior-grade bricks, or engineering bricks, both of which are harder than ordinary bricks, with low rates of water absorption and good frost resistance.

CONSIDERATIONS

To pave a surface more cheaply, you can use concrete "brick" pavers instead of clay bricks. They will not look as good as clay bricks, but they do the job. If you use clay bricks, you have a choice of laying them either frog face down, or stretcher face up. Bear this in mind when you work out the brick pattern and coverage.

BRICK PATTERNS

There are many traditional patterns for brick paving (originally called "floor" patterns), some dating back over 400 years. These classic patterns look just as good today.

Running wall bond

Square herringbone bond

Basketweave bond

Running and stack bond

Double basketweave bond

Diagonal herringbone bond

BRICKWORK ADDITIONS

The wonderful thing about building a brickwork patio is the ease of making additions to the project at a later date. If the patio has a good concrete foundation, you can furnish it with other brick structures such as boundary walls, pillars, raised borders, seats, a barbecue or even a raised pond.

Calculating brick quantities

If you lay the bricks stretcher face up (8 x 2 ¼ in), there are five bricks to every square foot. If you lay them frog face down (8 x 3 ⅝ in), there are three bricks to every square foot.

A standard clay brick plus joints is 8 ⅜ in long, 4 in wide and 2 ¼ in thick.

BRICK COMBINATIONS

Bricks are adaptable – they look equally good when they are combined with other materials such as clay tiles, concrete slabs, natural stone, cobbles and wood.

Old bricks with stone slabs and tiles

A formal pattern of bricks with an infill of cobbles, gravel and planting

A curved sweep of bricks combined with an infill of fine pea gravel and sand

A brick raised bed, built directly on the edge of the patio, creates a unified theme. It provides some shelter as well as a planting area.

HOW TO LAY A BRICK PATIO ON SOFT GROUND

If your site is wet and generally spongy and uneven, it is best to lay the bricks on a slab of concrete. This is hard work and adds to the cost of the project, but the concrete will ensure a long-lasting patio, and allows you to build additions without worrying about a foundation.

Buy ready-mixed concrete (or at least rent a cement mixer – refer to page 12), and recruit some friends to help you with the work.

Step 2
Spread a layer of compacted gravel over the whole site.

Step 3
Cover the gravel with a layer of concrete. Strike it level with the formwork boards.

Edge detail (cross-section)

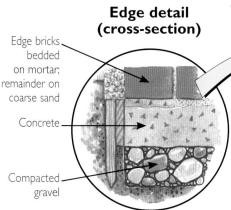

Edge bricks bedded on mortar; remainder on coarse sand

Concrete

Compacted gravel

Step 1
Remove the turf and topsoil. Dig down to a depth required by local code. Ring the site with formwork (planks to shape the concrete).

Step 4
Set the bricks on dry coarse sand. Ease and tap them level. Fill the joints with dry sand.

HOW TO LAY A CONCRETE PAVER PATIO ON FIRM, DRY GROUND

If the ground is firm and dry, you may choose to use concrete block pavers to cut costs. These can be laid directly on a bed of sand. An edging is necessary to prevent the pavers from spreading outwards.

Remove the turf and dig down to a depth required by local code. Shovel a line of stiff concrete around the site and set the edging pavers in position. Use a plank and level to ensure that the edging is level – both along the run of the edges and across the site.

Spread a mixture of fine topsoil and gravel and use a plate compacter to compact it to a level finish. Spread 2 in of coarse sand over the gravel and compact it to a smooth, level finish. Spread a thin layer of loose sand over the site and arrange the pavers so that they are about ½ in higher than the edging. Compact the pavers. Finally, spread fine sand over the paving and run the plate compacter over the whole site.

Cross-section

Earth dug out to a depth required by local code

Compacted earth and gravel

Retaining edge blocks set level in concrete

½ in of compacted coarse sand

Types of block and block patterns

Running wall bond – with joints staggered

Simple stacked side-by-side bond

Double basketweave bond

Herringbone bond set square

Herringbone bond set diagonally

Running hexagon 1-to-2 bond

Edges

Bricks set upright to make a strong soldier edge

Bricks set flat down to make a header course edge

Bricks set at an angle to make dog-tooth or Sussex edging

Bullnose bricks set upright to make a decorative edge

Decking patios

Can I make a large decking patio on several levels?

Decking is very versatile – it can be used to make a straightforward ground-level patio, or it can easily be built on several levels, like a seaside pier above water, or a forest observation platform. The advantage of decking is the speed of the whole building operation. An area of rugged ground can be swiftly transformed by a decking patio. If you want to build a dramatic patio without too much site disturbance, and you are in a hurry, decking is the answer.

The perfect decking patio, perched high above the ground in order to accommodate the site, take advantage of a beautiful woodland view, and facilitate birdwatching.

ADVANTAGES AND DISADVANTAGES

Advantages of a decking patio

✔ The site does not need levelling – posts of different lengths cope with the slope of the ground.

✔ The materials are easier to handle than those for a concrete slab patio.

✔ It can be built over utilities (water, gas and electricity lines).

✔ Generally, the materials aren't as invasive as brick and concrete.

Disadvantages of a decking patio

✘ With care, wooden decking can last for 25 years, but a brick patio will last for several lifetimes.

✘ Decking patios require a lot of maintenance – washing, treating, and general running repairs.

Grooved decking

Grooved decking is readily available in Europe, where it is favored because it is considered to be an anti-slip surface. In the USA, however, it is something of a rarity and only available by special order.

DECKING DESIGN OPTIONS

Attached to house

↗ *This patio has been raised above the ground so that it relates to the house.*

Separate from house

↗ *A deck built close to the water's edge, so that it can be used as an observation pier.*

Split-level

↗ *Decks raised one above another to step over an old foundation.*

Customized shape

↗ *Decking can be built to almost any shape.*

Patterned

↗ *The wood can be fixed in a variety of patterns.*

Cut-out area

↗ *Decking built to take advantage of a special tree.*

Individual

↗ *Decking designed as an eye-catching feature, to mirror an existing circular stone patio and a large, round millstone.*

BASIC DECKING CONSTRUCTION SEQUENCE

1 Prepare the ground

Measure out the plan view. Post positions will be determined by the size of decking, joists, beams and posts. Consult a local building authority to vet your plan.

6 Steps or balustrade?

If the decking is higher than 7 ½ in off the ground, you will need steps. Most local authorites have a building code that describes when a balustrade should be included (it is preferable if the decking is more than two steps high).

5 Cover with decking

Decking boards can be laid lengthwise, crosswise or diagonally. The simplest method is to lay them at right angles to the joists, with board lengths selected at random, so end joints are staggered.

Take a board, set it in place so that one end is centered on a joist, and then mark and cut the other end so that it centers on the nearest joist. Continue across the frame.

4 Build the inner frame

Position the joists within the beam frame according to local code. Code will specify how close the joists need to be together depending on the size of the joists and the decking above. Typically the joists are secured at each end by "joist hangers," metal brackets that reinforce the connection between beams and joists. Consult your local building inspector to get the relevant distances and necessary hardware.

2 Fix the posts

Dig holes to a depth set by local code and pour in a bit of gravel. Set posts in the holes and prop them so they are plumb. Fill the holes with concrete to just above the ground. Use a trowel to angle the top edge of the concrete so that the slope will throw off the rain.

3 Build the beam frame

Cut and fit the beams to make an outer frame that runs from post to post. Tack the beams in place, check with the carpenter level and make adjustments. Secure the frame at each beam–post intersection with ½ in-diameter stainless-steel nuts, bolts and washers.

DECKING BOARD PATTERNS

Some people like plain decking, while others prefer a more complicated design. As a general rule, a pattern of decking boards uses more timber and takes more time; however, the two parquet herringbone designs below show that an interesting pattern can be achieved simply by doubling up the joists at the point where the board ends are fixed.

Angled 45° to the run of the joists

Square-cut herringbone with doubled joists

Angle-cut zigzag with doubled joists

Large-module checkerboard parquet

Parallel to the house and at right angles to the joists

Single large diamond with doubled joists

Although designs involving a pattern of boards are expensive and time-consuming, you can speed up the work and keep wastage to a minimum simply by using an electric miter saw (chop saw).

BALUSTRADE

If your decking patio is more than a couple of steps off the ground, you need to fit a balustrade (sometimes called a railing) for safety reasons. A balustrade will completely transform the look of the decking, making it more of a focal point.

It is possible to build a perfectly good add-on balustrade to a patio, with all the members fixed to the main ring beam or fascia, but it is best to consider the structure at the initial design stage. For example, in the design pictured above, the balustrade posts are simply an extension of the main support posts, giving a structure that is both stable and strong. Integral posts such as these are safer than an add-on option.

A balustrade with integral posts, fretted boards, a top rail and decorative finials.

STEPS

If decking is more than 7 ½ mm high, it will need steps (or one or more small decking platforms). Try to design steps to relate to the design of the balustrade. (See page 60.)

Maintenance

Sweep up debris and make sure that all parts of the structure are ventilated, so that the wood remains dry. (See page 41.)

Decorative patios

An area of concrete makes a perfectly good patio, which will be dry, firm and level. But if you cover the concrete with cobbles, you will lift it from a merely functional structure to something altogether more decorative. If some part of a form has no reason for its existence other than to be pleasing to the eye, it can be defined as decorative. There are lots of ways to make a decorative patio by using various materials, patterns, planting and ornaments.

THINGS TO CONSIDER

Pattern and style

↗ Select a pattern and style that complement the design and location of your home. Just as you might theme a room in the house in a certain color, and use particular shapes or forms, apply the same principles to the patio.

Feasibility

↗ Even if you are very keen on a certain type of material, it may not be feasible to use it for an entire patio, for example if the cost is prohibitive. If that is the case, consider using a small number of units within the design to create a feature.

Practicalities

↗ Above all else, a patio must be comfortable underfoot and safe. For example, large cobbles are beautiful and hardwearing, but are they going to feel too lumpy? Glass is very attractive, but is it going to be dangerous for children?

DECORATIVE PATIO OPTIONS

Brick and stone combinations

↗ This is a classic, traditional mixture of old bricks and stone, perfect for an old house in the town or country. The bricks are ideal for patterning between the stones. Another idea is to leave out various stones, and use spaces as planting pockets. These look very effective when filled with low-growing rock garden plants such as house leeks, thyme and chamomile.

Cut stone and pot plants

↗ A patio made from cut stone decorated with an infill of plants – ideal for a small city garden.

Decorative patio kits

→ Patio kits can produce very predictable results, but it is possible to add an individualistic flourish. Accentuate the shape and add interest (also keep costs low) by trimming the patio kit with an infill of cobbles pressed into concrete.

Concrete and grass

↗ Plain concrete slabs decorated with ribbons of grass – an inexpensive option.

HOW TO MAKE A DECORATIVE PATIO USING CONCRETE SLABS

Choose a selection of concrete slabs, curbs, pavers and setts, all in the same muted color tone, and all much the same thickness.

Remove the grass and topsoil, and lay down a generous foundation of compacted gravel. Top with a slab of medium-strength concrete. Set the units on small blobs of mortar. Fill the joints with a dryish mix of mortar.

Step 4
When the mortar has set, brush and trowel a crumbly, dryish mix of mortar into the wide joints. Finally, spray the whole patio with a fine mist of water. Leave for at least 48 hours.

Step 3
Starting with the main design framework (the outer edge of the inner design), set each slab on four or five small blobs of mortar. Adjust the thickness of the mortar to accommodate variations in the thickness of the different slabs and setts. Allow generous joints between the slabs.

Step 2
Top the gravel with concrete. Tamp it down with a board, making a very slight, almost imperceptible fall to one side to allow rainwater to run off easily.

Step 1
Remove the turf and topsoil to a depth required by local code. Fill with compacted, levelled gravel.

HOW TO MAKE A PATCHWORK SLATE MOSAIC PATIO

Step 3
Lay the pieces of slate (dry) and arrange them for best fit and decorative effect. Check lines and angles with a straight-edge and a set square. Use a piece of chalk to mark out a guide grid for laying the slate.

Step 4
Starting with the main elements of the design, bed the slate in mortar. Check each piece with a carpenter's level.

Step 5
When the mortar is dry and the slate is firm underfoot, fill the joints with a waterproof grout. Sponge grout off the surface of the slate.

↙ Start by selecting rectilinear pieces of real slate in different colors and textures. If possible, work out a design that avoids the need to cut the slate; if it is unavoidable, only make straight cuts. Lay down a gravel foundation topped with a concrete slab. Arrange the pieces of slate dry, spending time achieving best fit. Finally, set the slate on a skim of mortar.

Step 2
Top the gravel with 4 in of concrete, striking it with a slight slope that will allow rainwater to run off. Use a metal float to skim the concrete to a smooth finish.

Step 1
Lay a foundation of 4 in of compacted gravel.

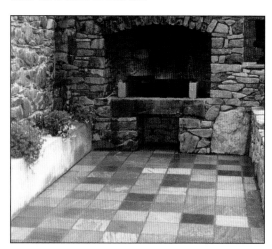

This alternative patchwork design consists of a mixture of slate and reconstituted stone, and incorporates an integral barbecue.

Split-level patios

If your garden is sloping, covered with old concrete foundations, or in any way less than level, you will need to create level areas if you want a place to sit, or somewhere for the children to play. One of the easiest ways of creating horizontal areas in a sloping garden is to build a split-level patio. Also, in a very flat and rather boring garden, a split-level patio can provide a high-rise room, which gives exciting views across the garden.

EXAMPLES OF SPLIT-LEVEL PATIOS

↗ *If you want to create a beautiful, long-lasting, traditional split-level patio, with steps, terraces, flagstones, random stone raised beds and planting areas, real stone is the answer.*

→ *Bricks look equally good in a city backyard or in a cottage garden. They are easy to obtain, available in many different colors and textures, light to handle and easy to work with.*

↗ *Decking is a great way of building a split-level patio. It doesn't require big foundations or retaining walls: you simply build a series of platforms or steps at different levels.*

SPLIT-LEVEL PATIO CONSTRUCTION DETAILS

→ When you are building a split-level patio in brick, you are in effect constructing one or more giant terraces or steps. If the ground is soft or crumbly, you need to build retaining walls to hold back the earth and to support the weight of the horizontal paving. All the walls need to be built on a traditional gravel and concrete foundation.

→ The walls of a split-level stone patio must be built on a gravel and concrete foundation. High walls need to be buttressed to provide extra support (wider at the base than the top, with a vertical inside face and an angled outside face). Get professional help with this.

Brick

Brick or stone coping to protect the top of the wall

A well bonded, two-brick-thick wall

Opening in course for weep-hole drainage

Compacted gravel and concrete foundation slab under the brick pavers

Coarse backfill with drainage pipe

Compacted gravel and concrete foundation slab

Stone

Compacted gravel and concrete foundation slab under the paving slabs

Backfill of loose gravel for swift drainage

Concrete foundation slab on compacted hardcore

Split-level decking

If you want to build a split-level patio without too much disturbance to the site, or if you enjoy working with wood, rather than brick or stone, or you want the job done fast, decking is the answer. (See pages 34–35.)

Circular patios

Primitive man thought that the circle was a magical symbol, and circular patios have a timeless quality that somehow makes them special. Perhaps it is the perfect symmetry of circles that makes them so attractive. They also provide an excellent opportunity for creating a pattern in different colors and materials, to make a striking motif. If you want to build a patio that makes an eye-catching feature, consider trying one of these.

Why choose a circular patio?

CIRCULAR PATIO OPTIONS

Paved circle (patio kit)	Decorative combination	Circle in a square or rectangle	Decking (and polygons)	More options

➚ There are lots of circular paver kits on the market – perfect for an instant patio.

➚ Bricks and stone setts are a traditional combination, but there are many others.

➚ A round flagstone feature in a square patio makes an exciting geometrical mix.

➚ Not quite a circle, but a decking polygon (a hexagon or octagon) is the next best thing.

You could make a cobbled circle with a millstone at its center, or a series of circular decking patios at different levels. A patio made entirely out of old bricks would be distinctive (however this involves a lot of work and is quite difficult to build. (See page 9.)

POSITIONING CIRCULAR PATIOS

Position a comfortable chair in a likely spot and relax with a cup of coffee. Does the site feel right? If so, mark out the circle with sand (see page 14) and see how it relates to the rest of the garden. Live with it for a few days before committing.

Sun and shade balance
Find a sheltered, sunny spot, with just the right amount of shade – perhaps from a nearby tree.

Sloping sites
If the site is steeply sloped, think about a split-level patio – perhaps a series of terraces or an area of raised decking with steps.

Visibility
Do you want the patio to be a hideaway, out of view of the house, or do you want it to be a focal point?

Access to the house
Do you want the patio close to the house, like a linked room, so that you can move directly from the house to the patio?

HOW TO BUILD A CIRCULAR CRAZY-PAVING PATIO

➜ ⭹ Scribe out the circle (see page 14), and remove the turf and topsoil to a depth required by code. Fill with compacted gravel for a solid base and top with sand. Fit a small area (dry) so that you know how to place the pieces. Set the stones on a generous layer of a dryish mix of concrete. Point the gaps with mortar.

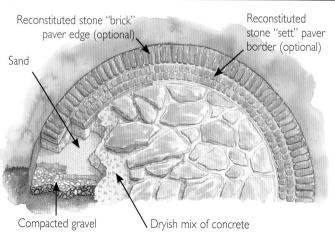

Reconstituted stone "brick" paver edge (optional)

Reconstituted stone "sett" paver border (optional)

Sand

Compacted gravel

Dryish mix of concrete

Patio edgings

Why do patios need to be edged?

Patios need edging for three reasons: structure, decoration and practicality. At the structural level, an edging contains a patio – without it, the patio would slowly ooze, spread and self-destruct under its own weight. At the decorative level, an edging defines a patio, like a frame around a picture. At the practical level, an edging stops grass or flowers from invading a patio, making it easier to keep the garden neat and in good order.

WHAT IS A PATIO EDGING?

A patio edging can be anything from a row of bricks hidden away just below the surface of the ground, to a decorative wall complete with integral raised borders, pillars, seating, a barbecue and planting.

The type you choose depends upon the size, site and materials of the patio, but you also need to decide (at the design stage) whether the edging is to be a highly visible feature, or whether it can do its job hidden from view.

PATIO WALLS

A stone wall topped with slabs makes a beautiful, traditional edging that is handy for seating, or for displaying plants.

If you have the time and money, you can extend and enlarge an edging into a wall that can become a dynamic structure in its own right, such as a seat or a raised bed.

If your patio has a drop of two or more steps between it and the ground, it requires a safety barrier. You could build a wall that is both a balustrade to prevent you falling off, and a visually exciting decorative feature.

PATIO EDGING OPTIONS

Quick edgings

Wooden board nailed to stakes and driven into the ground

Round-nosed quarry tiles two-thirds buried in the ground

Ready-made log roll strip, half-buried in the ground

Bricks set end to end and half-buried in the ground

← If the ground is firm and the patio relatively small and lightweight in structure, you can create a quick edging simply by half-burying bricks, wood or tiles in a shallow trench.

Zigzag brick edgings

Bricks all set at an angle

Bricks set lower than the grass

← A row of zigzag bricks set at an angle in mortar, with a row of bricks set flat down to one side, makes the perfect edge between a patio and a lawn. Mowing is easy – a lawnmower can be pushed hard up against the zigzag bricks.

Mini brick wall edgings

→ This is the perfect edging when you want to create a strong division between the patio and the lawn. The wall is built on a concrete foundation, and some part of the wall is buried below ground. The trench between the wall and the lawn is filled with gravel to hold back the lawn.

Trench filled with gravel

Brick wall on a concrete foundation

Railing and safety

If you have a patio that is a couple of steps higher than a lawn, you can surround it with a decorative wall if you wish. However, if the patio is raised higher than 30 in, a railing is compulsory for safety reasons – the local planning authority would insist on a railing of at least 42 in. If your site is exposed, you are worried about children's safety, or you want privacy, you can design the railing so that it doubles as a screen.

This wooden railing also acts as screen around a raised patio.

Maintenance

It is no good walking out on to your patio on the first day of spring and expecting it to be in tip-top condition and ready to use, if you have ignored it since the summer. It will be covered in debris, the woodwork might well be green and slimy, and all the cracks and crannies will be full of bugs. A patio needs to be kept in order with a program of regular maintenance, with tasks to carry out before and after each season of patio use.

What does maintenance involve? Is it necessary?

BASIC PATIO MAINTENANCE

In early spring, at the end of summer and just before winter, carry out tasks concerned with maintaining the surface of the patio. Also keep an eye on the condition of patio additions such as containers, walls, trellises, water features, lighting and barbecues.

Concrete paver and slab maintenance

Removing weeds and moss
Don't let these invasive plants get a hold: remove them as soon as they appear. Dig out rather than using weedkiller.

Gap filling
Clean all the debris from the gaps and fill them either with sand or a dry, crumbly mortar made with fine sand and cement.

Efflorescence
There are four ways to tackle a patio that shows a white deposit called efflorescence: you can brush it off every time it appears, you can use a proprietary remover, you can wash it with vinegar, or you can leave it alone (it looks unsightly but is harmless).

Cleaning pavers
Sweep up debris and scrub with soapy water. Bleach or special cleaners, together with a hose or pressure spray, will help wash off algae.

Replacing broken pavers
If the paver is cracked, whack it with a hammer and use an old chisel to ease the fragments clear. Remove old mortar and debris from the recess. Check that the replacement paver is a good fit and then bed it in sand or mortar. Fill the joints to match.

MAINTAINING BRICKS AND CONCRETE PAVERS

Early every spring, brick and paver patios need a good wash and scrub. Use an old knife or chisel to scrape the joints clear of weeds and ants, and sweep up the debris. Scrub the surface with soapy water and mop dry. If the surface is green or slimy, add a small amount of bleach to the water. If you want a sheen or shiny finish to the surface, brush it with a proprietary finish or sealant.

MAINTAINING REAL STONE

Apart from regular brushing, a real stone patio is best left to develop a patina. If the patina presents a danger (for instance if the surface is breaking away, or it is slippery underfoot), you need to tackle it each season. Sweep up debris and mop down the patio with water containing a little bleach. Clean old and cracked mortar from the joints and repair with mortar (1 part cement, 6 parts soft sand, 1 part lime).

OTHER MAINTENANCE TIPS

The best single tip is to keep the patio well swept. On the face of it, this does not sound very efficacious, but the sweeping process both helps prevent trouble and reveals problems at an early stage. For example, it gets rid of piles of leaves, which might house vermin or become slippery underfoot, it disposes of ants' nests, and it discloses broken slabs and cracked mortar. If you discover a small problem after sweeping, sort it out before it gets bigger and more difficult to remedy.

MAINTAINING DECKING PATIOS

If wooden decking is sturdily built and well looked after and maintained, it will last about 25 years. The biggest danger is moisture. If the wood is well ventilated, it doesn't matter if it gets soaked when it rains, then dries out in the sun and wind, but if it is constantly damp, the wood will soon break down under insect attack and various molds. The best defence is to sweep up debris, remove algae with soap and water, and then let the decking dry. Do this in spring and autumn.

If existing decking is a poor, softwood construction, the best thing to do is to protect it with garden paint. (If you are about to build some decking, either use a top-quality hardwood, or a special pressure-treated softwood.)

Revitalizing existing patios

Can I do anything about my terrible patio?

Most patios can be reborn if you lavish a little time, money and effort on them. Small patios can be enlarged, ugly concrete patios can be covered over, cracked concrete pavers can be lifted and replaced, old bricks can be enhanced, boring patios can be embellished with features and planting or furnished with new furniture, and so on. If you are fed up with your existing patio, it can definitely be given a facelift.

HOW TO TRANSFORM A DULL PATIO

BEFORE

WHAT MAKES A PATIO LOOK DULL?

If a patio is uninspiring, it is often due to neglect. Old plastic furniture is pushed to one side, broken pots are left in corners, weeds are allowed to grow through it, and so on. Once a patio becomes a dumping ground, nobody will want to use it – sitting outside in an unloved area, surrounded by junk, is unappealing. But a patio that gets lots of use is never dull – the seats are comfortable and dry, and it is generally an attractive place where people want to spend time. (See patio maintenance on page 41.)

Furniture

Choose comfortable patio furniture: chairs or a bench and perhaps sun loungers. You will also need a table. If you don't want to have to bring furniture indoors when it rains, select the material accordingly. (See page 64.)

Planting

Just as you might embellish a room in your home with pictures on the wall and curtains at the windows, a garden room – your patio – benefits from being embellished with plants. Groups of ferns around a water feature, a collection of bonsai trees, a raised bed planted with graceful grasses, one or more really spectacular plants – there are lots of possibilities. If your patio is slightly sheltered, it can be used as a nursery area for seedlings. (See page 68.)

Type of surface

There is nothing quite so dull and depressing as a bald patch of gray concrete. It will last forever, but after a year or two you might very well begin to wish that it would just go away. But then again, concrete makes a perfect base for bricks. Genuine rustic bricks look great and are particularly good in a country garden. If the bricks are old and slightly bruised at the corners, so much the better. (See page 32.)

AFTER

Lighting

Nothing improves a patio more quickly than low-level spotlights positioned to pick out special features. (See page 79.)

Water features

There is something rather comforting about sitting on a patio and enjoying the sights and sounds of moving water. A water feature doesn't have to be anything large or dramatic – a small waterspout set in a wall, gently bubbling and splashing into a pool, is ideal and something that children can safely enjoy. (See page 77.)

Ornaments and sculpture

A sculpture or ornament will liven up a dull corner – perhaps a ceramic cat, a boot scraper doorstop, a gnome, a collection of ceramic tiles or some old tools. (See page 72.)

The addition of a pergola provides some privacy and shade, as well as giving a new dimension to a straightforward patio. A large, striking urn injects drama.

EXTENDING A PATIO

Extending a paved area

There is no reason why a patio cannot be extended on one or all sides. It is better not to try and match the existing materials, because products change in size and style over the years, but rather to look at it as a chance to brighten up the whole patio by framing it with new and exciting materials.

For example, you could frame an existing concrete paver patio with bricks, real stone, or concrete slabs in a different color. Measure the existing patio, decide on the preferred size of the units, bricks or slabs, and then search out new materials that fit into this scheme.

More unusual ways of extending a paved area

← An existing patio can be slowly extended by making gradual additions to the sides. First, for example, you could add a small area of concrete studded with cobbles. This might be supplemented by some roundel (circular) slabs and more cobbles interspersed with planting.

Extending decking

→ Wooden decking can be extended by building another deck at one side. To add interest, do not build it on the same level and to the same shape. Instead, alter the shape, skew it slightly and make it several steps higher. A small platform will make a step between the two.

IS THE PATIO IN THE WRONG PLACE?

Over time, things change – trees grow taller, neighbors might build an intrusive extension that cuts out the sunlight, a road might become bigger and noisier, and so on – all factors that might spoil your enjoyment of a once-comfortable patio. If this happens, consider all the possibilities. Would it be sensible to move the patio slightly and reuse part of the old foundation? Could you lift the whole thing and reuse all the materials? If you built a screen to one side to add privacy or to protect you from an obtrusive view, would it improve matters? Could you prune a tree to let in more sunlight?

If none of these options is feasible, the existing patio is too small and not quite in the right place, or you have moved to a new house and you don't like the patio, you might as well write it off and start over again. However, don't be in too much of a hurry to do this, because there is always the chance that with a lot of lateral thinking, other possibilities will present themselves.

Before you remove an old patio, consider whether it could be used for a new purpose, such as a children's play area, or as a base for a new workshop. If the materials cannot be reclaimed intact, perhaps they can be put to good use as recycled materials elsewhere.

REUSING A FOUNDATION

If you like the position of your patio and are only going to increase its size slightly, there is no reason why you cannot reuse part of the old foundation. All you do is lay an additional concrete slab to the side of the original one, and build the patio extension.

COVERING A PATIO

Sometimes a patio is perfectly positioned and just the right size, but not very attractive to look at. If this is the case, simply cover it over with a new material. Remove all the features and materials that are worth saving, and make good the patio surface with extra concrete. Build the surrounding edging slightly higher, and then cover the whole patio with bricks or decking. (See pages 32–35.)

Choosing paths and steps

Paths look fairly easy; are steps difficult to do?

Most beginners are happy enough building paths and wooden steps, but are worried about the prospect of building a flight of traditional steps (such as a run of three brick steps), often because they cannot visualize or understand the order of work. Steps are built from the bottom tread upwards. In essence, all you do is build a series of little platforms, with each successive platform or tread raised and offset from its neighbor.

OPTIONS FOR PATHS AND STEPS

Gravel and logs

↑ The perfect steps for a country garden: logs or risers set the height of the steps and create a feature, and compacted pea gravel is used for the treads.

Stone

↑ Traditional stone steps made from a mixture of cut stone for the risers, step nosings and side walls, and crazy paving for the treads.

Decorative

↑ A beautiful flight of courtyard steps, with terracotta tiles for both risers and treads. These steps would look great in a small, walled town garden.

Wooden

↑ A flight of steps made entirely from reclaimed railroad ties – a long-lasting, easy-to-build option, suitable for a country or city garden.

Brick and tile

↑ Traditional brick and tile steps. The bricks are set on edge to make the risers, and tiles are used to make a decorative feature out of the treads.

PLANNING PATHS AND STEPS IN THE GARDEN

A formal garden layout (plan view)

Straight lines
As far as possible, the paths run in straight lines parallel to the sides of the garden. There are no wandering curves or free bends.

Symmetry
Paths and steps aligned and centered with both the house and the garden. Steps lead from the patio, and a path runs down the garden.

Geometry
If the path needs to change direction, it must do so at right angles, using squares or circles at important junctions.

Pattern
Subtle pattern arrangements created in traditional materials (stone, bricks, cobbles and tiles), not brightly colored tiles or paint.

An informal garden layout (plan view)

↗ Try to foster the impression that the garden has been created over many years. Avoid drawing formal plans, stay away from designs that are geometric and symmetrical, and generally let designs evolve to suit changing needs. Encourage paths to meander around the garden, just as people might wander from one area to another.

Quick paths and steps

It is quite possible to make a path and a flight of steps in the space of a couple of weekends, by spending the first weekend planning the operation, and the second building. It will be hard work: the building weekend will involve long days, and you will need help, but provided that there is good weather, it is possible to complete a project in this timespan. Some of the more complicated projects may require a little concrete.

Can I build quickly without a lot of concrete?

QUICK PATHS

Gravel
➜ *A gravel path is quick to make. Clear the turf and topsoil, spread 4 in of compacted gravel, cover with landscape fabric, and top with 4 in of gravel. Edge the path with large rocks.*

Stepping stones
➜ *Stepping stones are great for an informal garden. Dig out the turf; bed the stones on sand.*
↘ *You can create an instant, winding path with decking "stepping stones" – remove the turf and set the circles in place.*

Wooden walkway
↘ *Wooden walkways suit a country garden and also make a fine path to complement decking. Use pressure-treated wood. To make a walkway, put two parallel wooden rails directly on the ground and nail boards in place across them. If the site is wet, you can set the rails on concrete blocks.*

More ideas
- Try a path made from salvaged telegraph poles, boards and gravel (illustrated right).
- Crushed tree bark makes an instant, biodegradable path, which is perfect for a traditional country cottage garden.
- A mixture of crushed stone and coarse sand makes an instant path.

QUICK STEPS

Post and bark
➜ *Log posts, staked in place, define the width of the steps; thicker logs decide step height and the spacing of the treads. The treads are lined with landscape fabric and topped with bark or gravel.*

Wooden plank steps
➜ *Traditional steps with open risers, side boards and plank treads. All the joints can be made using metal angle plates – a really good option for porch steps or steps leading to an area of decking.*

Decking steps
➜ *Broad decking steps can be built to cover existing steps – useful for improving mean, narrow steps, or when you want to build wide steps to give easy and safe access for children or older people.*

More ideas
- You could build a flight of steps using concrete blocks stacked and mortared together.
- You could look for a steps "kit" in a reclamation yard: part of an old cast-iron fire escape or spiral staircase.
- Logs and planks make good steps.
- A series of wooden platforms, at slightly different heights and set side by side, would make shallow steps.
- Stacked concrete blocks, mortared together, with reconstituted stone slabs on top, make sturdy steps.

Basic paths

How do I make a path from house to patio?

Some people live in a house for years, continually wishing that they had paths running to the lawn, vegetable garden or patio, and yet they don't do anything about it because they think that paths are complex structures to build. However, there are lots of ways to create a basic path, some of which are very simple. The process does not even have to involve lots of heavy digging – gravel or stepping stones are two very uncomplicated options.

IDEAS FOR BASIC PATHS

Gravel path

A traditional path made from pea gravel – its crunchy texture is enjoyable to walk on.

Concrete path

Concrete paths are straightforward to make and can last for hundreds of years.

Brick path

A traditional red brick path laid in a herringbone pattern – perfect for a cottage garden.

Stepping-stone path

Large, weathered slabs of real stone make delightful stepping stones across a lawn.

A GRAVEL PATH

A path made from pea gravel is one of the easiest types of path to lay, and the sound of gravel underfoot is a joy. Remove the turf, dig down to a depth of about 6 in, edge the path with boards, spread a layer of compacted gravel and top this with pea gravel. If the ground is dry, just remove the turf, put down a sheet of landscape fabric and spread the gravel.

Step 4
Spread 3 in of pea gravel over the gravel, then roll and press it to a smooth finish.

Step 3
Spread gravel and stamp it down to a compacted finish, 3 in thick.

Step 2
Edge both sides of the path with boards set flush with the ground.

Step 1
Remove the turf and dig down to a depth of 6 in (deeper if the ground is wet).

A CONCRETE PATH

A narrow, straight-as-an-arrow concrete path is very appealing in its simplicity. First, remove the turf and dig down to a depth of about 6 in. Edge the path with a board, spread 3 in of compacted gravel, and top it with 3 in of tamped concrete.

Trench dug to a depth of 6 in

Path edged with 3 in-wide boards

Boards allow for concrete expansion

Compacted gravel (3 in thick)

Concrete (3 in thick)

Boards set across the path every 1 yd

MORE BASIC PATHS

A path can be as basic as you wish – for example stepping stones, crushed stone, shingle, crushed shell, crushed tree bark, concrete blocks, cobbles or pebbles embedded in mortar. If you can come up with a material that is long-lasting and firm, dry and non-slippery underfoot, it will serve as a path. If the ground is hard you can build straight on top of it, but if it is wet, you need to remove the turf and topsoil, lay and compact gravel, and stop the path from spreading by edging it with boards or bricks.

Natural paths

Anatural path is a more informal type of path that attempts to recreate a look from nature. At heart, it is a strip of more or less level land that is dry and comfortable underfoot – and by replicating woody, stony, shingly or sandy conditions, you can build a path that perhaps paints a picture of hiking through mountains, exploring a mysterious forest, pottering around a seaside haunt or crossing imposing desert scenery.

How do I make a path that doesn't look manmade?

Stepping stones casually meander across a sea of pea gravel planted with species that enjoy well-drained conditions, such as rock plants, grasses and plants of Mediterranean origin.

CHOOSING A THEME

Once you have decided to build a natural path, you need to analyze which features define your chosen example. For instance, a real shoreline beach path is made up of pebbles and sand, and there may be larger water-washed stones and scattered pieces of driftwood lying about. These characteristics need to be incorporated into your design, so that they instantly transport the path user to that environment.

CHOOSE A PRACTICAL OPTION

Try to match the envisaged path to your existing garden. You might want a beach path, but if your garden is damp, with a clay soil and lush plants, and a dense tree canopy, a beach path might look rather out of place.

MAINTENANCE

A natural path will, to a greater or lesser extent, need regular maintenance – leaves removing, topping up with pebbles or bark, the edges tending, and so on – just like any other path.

HOW TO CREATE A NATURAL-LOOKING WOODLAND PATH

The characteristics of a woodland path are that it is dry and soft underfoot, and snakes around trees, wet areas and the occasional rock or fallen tree, with the width of the path changing to suit the terrain.

Look at your garden and find the best way of routing the path to take in existing features, such as a pond or trees. Use stakes and string to mark out the route. Clear the turf and remove the soil to a depth of about 6 in. Put 3 in of compacted gravel in the trench and top it with a sheet of woven weed-stop plastic. Cover this with a mixture of crushed bark, wood chips and leaf mold. Position feature rocks at the side, plus a large log or tree trunk that is big enough to sit on. Plant ferns, bluebells, bushes and scrub trees on both sides of the path.

Step 4
Plant ferns, bushes and scrub trees alongside the path. Encourage wild woodland flowers and climbing plants.

Step 3
Cover the gravel with landscape fabric topped with bark, wood chips and leaf mold. Position feature rocks and a tree trunk.

Step 2
Remove the turf and topsoil to a depth of 6 in. Lay 3 in of compacted gravel.

Step 1
Use stakes and string to route the path around various existing garden features. Vary the width of the path.

Brick or paver paths

Brick paths are time-consuming to make, but not difficult. After removing turf and topsoil from the site and completing the basic structures as for any other path, you are faced with the task of laying the bricks. However, in their favor, bricks are handy and comfortable to work with, there is something uniquely interesting about the way they fit together, and at the end of the project you will have a path that lasts a lifetime.

A basketweave brick path makes an attractive, practical division between flower borders, and is a particularly good option for a cottage garden.

A wide brick path provides a useful dry area between the house and garden, and allows easy mowing of the lawn. Its width means there is enough space for substantial planters.

A diagonal herringbone path bordered by cobbles set in mortar. Clay pavers have been selected in a range of colors to give an interesting twist to a traditional design.

TYPES OF CLAY BRICK

For garden projects, it is best to use well-fired (or high-fired) exterior-grade bricks, or engineering bricks, both of which are harder than ordinary bricks, with low rates of water absorption and good frost resistance. Reclaimed bricks may be available from an architectural salvage company.

Avoid new bricks manufactured to look like old – the decorative face will abrade if used on a path, and they can only be used stretcher face uppermost.

New engineering brick – good for edgings

Old worn and weathered high-fired brick

BLOCK PAVERS

Pavers are extremely hard, thin clay or concrete bricks designed specifically for paths, patios and drives. They come in many shapes, sizes and finishes. Perhaps the most attractive and durable option is the kiln-fired, brick-sized clay paver, in subtle colors that never fade. Concrete pavers include imitation stone setts (small rectangular paving blocks) and mock bricks.

Genuine kiln-fired clay paver

Concrete pavers imitating stone setts

BRICK PATH CONSIDERATIONS

Bricks have two end or "header" faces, two side or "stretcher" faces, a top or "frog" face, and a bottom face. The pattern bricks are laid in is termed the bond. Consider how path style will affect costs.

Style ~ Brick paths are straight or gently curved, with bricks set frog face down or on their side (stretcher). Straight, narrow paths use the fewest bricks. Curved paths require bricks to be set on their side, so using more bricks and increasing costs.

Cost ~ You can cut costs by using concrete "brick" pavers, but these are a poor second to genuine clay bricks.

Number of cut bricks ~ Minimize costs and effort with a design that uses whole bricks rather than involving cutting.

Calculating brick quantities

1. Calculate the area ~ Measure the length and width of the path and multiply together to give the area.

2. Calculate the number of bricks ~ Lay out a few bricks in the desired pattern to fill a square foot or yard of space. Multiply that number by the total area.

3. Add 5% for wastage ~ If you reckon that you need 100 whole bricks, get 105.

PATTERNS FOR PATHS

There are two differences between clay bricks and concrete or clay pavers. Bricks can be laid with any face uppermost, but pavers can only be laid with the wide face uppermost. Also, brick sizes allow for wide joints, while pavers are designed to touch each other. Visit a builders' merchant to buy the bricks or pavers, laying out a few on the ground in the desired pattern to see how they look.

Mitered herringbone

↗ *Clay pavers laid in a traditional herringbone; mitered where they meet the edging. A tricky pattern with lots of cutting.*

Square herringbone

↗ *Clay pavers laid in a traditional square herringbone pattern that only requires bricks to be cut in half.*

Face-up basketweave

↗ *Bricks laid face up in a 3-by-3 basketweave pattern. This attractive, traditional design has no bricks to cut.*

Frog-down basketweave

↗ *Bricks laid frog face down in a 2-by-2 basketweave pattern that uses fewer bricks, has no bricks to cut, but is not so subtle.*

TURNING CORNERS

With brick or paver paths, corners are best turned at right angles, so that your chosen pattern can be interlocked at the turn. This herringbone pattern is turned simply by following through in a different direction, and there is no need to cut many bricks.

HOW TO MAKE A BRICK PATH

Mark out the route and width of the path. Remove the turf and topsoil to a depth of 6 in. Edge the path with wooden boards. Lay 3 in of compacted gravel. Set the edge bricks in mortar. Lay ¾ in of compacted ballast, ¾ in of compacted coarse sand and a thin layer of raked soft sand. Position the bricks, brush fine sand into the joints, and use a plate compacter to compact them level.

Step 6
Set the bricks in place. Brush sand into the joints.

Step 5
Put down about an inch of compacted coarse sand and a thin layer of soft sand.

Step 4
Put down a mixture of 1 ½ in of compacted sand and gravel.

Step 3
Mortar a row of bricks along each edge, so that it is level with the paths.

Step 1
Remove the turf and topsoil to a depth of 6 in. Edge the path with boards set level.

Step 2
Put down an 3 in-thick layer of compacted gravel.

CUTTING BRICKS

There are four ways of cutting a brick: you can give it a sharp blow with a mason's hammer, use a small sledge hammer with a brick chisel, get hold of an angle grinder, or rent a brick cutter (like a guillotine).

Brick chisel set on the line of cut

Brick supported on a piece of carpet

To use a brick chisel and small sledge hammer, set the chisel on the mark and give it serveral crisp blows with the hammer.

CUTS TO AVOID

It is easier to cut a brick in half across its length than it is to cut at an angle. If you make lots of mistakes trying to cut bricks at an angle, the project is going to work out to be more expensive (in time and money) than intended. For these two very good reasons, it is best for beginners to choose a pattern that minimizes the need to cut bricks.

Decorative paths

A path is primarily a utilitarian surface, but with added decoration, it can move beyond the merely functional. Designs can incorporate beautiful colors and textures, reveal patterns built up from the placement of various materials, or display motifs (reflecting a variety of imagery) stamped into concrete. The decoration can be in the edging or even the very shape of the path. The options for creativity are as broad as your imagination.

DESIGN AND INSPIRATION

Having first decided on the route of the path and its primary function, you need to look at what you can afford.

Let's say that you want a path to run from the back door of the house into the garden. It needs to be hardwearing and traditional. A red brick path laid out according to a traditional pattern is one solution. If, however, you would prefer a cheaper option, a gravel path with an edging made from salvaged bricks might be more appropriate.

Look at your house and garden, take into account your likes and dislikes, such as an antipathy for straight lines or a love of swirling patterns, and then draw inspiration from the color and texture of the site.

A path made from reconstituted stone slabs framed with cast "Celtic" pavers. There are many such pavers on the market.

Questions to ask yourself

Assess the purpose ~ Is the path to be purely functional – for example to go around the vegetables? Or is it to make a design statement in the garden? Select materials accordingly.

Choose an appropriate style ~ A path made from railroad ties might look good in a country garden, but how would it look in your city courtyard? Consider the proportion of the units in relation to their surroundings.

Think about the cost ~ Gravel is the cheapest and real stone flagstones are the most expensive. How much do you want to spend? Is money an issue?

Consider curves and bends ~ Curvy and winding paths are best made from small components such as gravel and bricks, which give flexibility in design.

SOME CLASSIC DECORATIVE PATH DESIGNS

DECORATIVE BRICK PATHS

Brick paths are one of the most traditional and the most flexible in design terms. In many ways, they are also the easiest to lay. Special engineering bricks or well-fired house bricks are used, which are harder than ordinary bricks and will not crumble. See page 48.

Crazy-paving path

A traditional crazy-paving path. Randomly shaped pieces of stone are set in mortar on a foundation of compacted gravel.

Cobble path

A cobble path with a single line of bricks on either edge. The cobbles are simply evenly spaced and pressed into mortar.

HOW TO MAKE A DECORATIVE PAVER PATH

➜ ↘ Today we have the choice of using pavers to make a path, rather than following the traditional method of using engineering bricks, well-fired house bricks, or salvaged bricks. Pavers are super-hard, thin bricks made from clay or concrete, which are specifically for use in the construction of paths, drives and patios. They come in many shapes and sizes, and various finishes – everything from simple brick lookalikes through to imitation stone. The path illustrated uses two types of paver: "brick" setts and "stone" tiles.

Step 1
Dig to a depth of 6 in and fill with a little more than 2 in of compacted gravel. Fill the remaining depth with concrete, leaving enough for the thickness of the pavers.

Step 2
Bed the border paver setts on mortar, ensuring that they are level and flush with the ground at the side of the path.

Step 3
Cut and fit the tile pavers and bed them in mortar - so that they are level and flush with the border paver setts.

Step 4
Set the edging tiles in place on mortar. Dig a slot trench and fill it with pea gravel (so that you can mow right up to the edge of the path).

Step 5
Use a small pointing trowel to fill the joints with a dryish mix of mortar. Carefully wipe the path clear of debris.

BRICKS AND SETTS

Traditional bricks are usually about twice the thickness of modern paver setts. If you want to mix the two to create a path, first lay the bricks in sand and then lay the setts. In the path illustrated below, the joints have been planted with grass seed so that grass will bind the bricks and setts together. The mower can be run straight over a path like this.

Paver setts bedded in sand and levelled with the bricks

Compacted coarse sand (4 in thick)

Bricks bedded and levelled in sand

COPING WITH CURVES

The trick to building a curved path is to use small units. The smaller the unit, the easier it is to create a curve. For example, a tight curve can be created by using small setts, or broken half-bricks positioned best end uppermost.

PROBLEMS WITH LEVELS

Before starting a project, decide what level you want the finished path to be. Do you want it to be flush with the surrounding ground, or at a higher level than it? Dig the foundation to suit. Adjust the depth of the gravel according to the desired results.

BE CREATIVE WITH A MOSAIC PATH

A mosaic path will provide an artistic challenge. You need a firm foundation consisting of 4 in of compacted gravel topped off with 3 in of concrete. Thicknesses of the compacted gravel and concrete are often dictated by local codes. Check with your local code office for the correct thicknesses in your area.

TEXTURAL PATTERN PATHS

A textural pattern takes its starting point from the character of the stone and evolves through the way the pieces of stone are laid down. Various textures of stone can be used to complement each other, or laid down in contrasting adjacent areas to underline the qualities of each material. From crazy paving to square slabs, cobbles or gravel, there are hundreds of options. Visit a builders' merchant for inspiration, then use your imagination to create an effective design.

Random slabs laid square to each other, with the joints filled with gravel.

Setts placed in a traditional, highly structured shell design.

Granite setts laid side by side according to best fit, in a traditional design.

Curved paths

I would like a curved path – are they complicated?

A meandering path with curvaceous bends is a wonderful sight. The complexity of the path depends on the materials used to build it. There is an old adage that says "spacing and placing is better than cutting" – it is much better to use materials that can be carefully spaced and placed to follow the line of the path, rather than to use a rigid grid of concrete slabs, for example, where the edge slabs need to be cut to fit the edge of the path.

SWEEPING CURVES

If the curve is big enough – for example a sweeping curve running over a distance of 20 yds – it can almost be treated like a straight line. Wood edging can be bent into position, even the joints in brick and slab paths can be eased, tweaked and angled so that the path runs round the curve. Never try cutting large numbers of slabs to fit the curve – it's a difficult task, and the resulting path will look lifeless.

PROBLEMS WITH CURVES

When using materials such as slabs and blocks to build a curved path, the tighter the curve involved, the greater the problems presented. You have two choices if you must build a tightly curved path: either use materials that can easily run around curves, such as bark, concrete, gravel, small pavers, cobbles set in concrete, or mosaic; or build it from thin materials such as slate, tiles or old bricks, which can be set on edge and fanned out so that they readily run around both convex and concave curves.

The sweeping curve of this path is so broad that it can be achieved by adjusting the mortar joints between the bricks, allowing them to run smoothly round the curve.

Choosing materials for building curved paths

Path-building materials under consideration for a curved path can be divided into three categories, according to degree of complexity. When using fixed modular materials such as bricks or slabs, the challenge is to make the path's surface appear to flex with the curves.

Easy

Spread materials can be poured and raked, providing a very easy solution.

Pea gravel ~ Pea gravel is a good, traditional option – just rake and roll it over a base of gravel. (See page 45.)

Crushed stone ~ Crushed stone can be treated in the same way as gravel.

Concrete ~ Concrete is a reliable option, especially if interest is added to the surface by patterning it with a brush, or studding with small pebbles.

Tree bark ~ Very easy to spread, firm underfoot and toddler-friendly. It can be put on the vegetable garden when it eventually breaks down.

Slightly more complex

The smaller the units chosen, the easier it makes the task.

Bricks ~ Old bricks, set on edge, can be arranged to fan around a curve. A very useful way of doing an edging.

Slate roof tiles ~ Broken roof tiles can be set in mortar so that only the edge shows. For a traditional checkerboard design, slices of slate are grouped and bedded in mortar in this way. Slates look especially good in combination with brick.

Cobbles ~ Cobbles are fun to use. They need a foundation of compacted gravel; mortar is spread on top and the cobbles bedded in place.

To be avoided

Stay away from large modules, because they are very difficult to lay.

Square slabs ~ The only easy way to use these is to set them down like stepping stones, and surround them with a material such as gravel.

Railroad ties ~ These are heavy and difficult to cut – not really suitable for an average narrow garden path.

Ceramic tiles ~ Ceramic tiles are best avoided unless you want to break them up and create a mosaic path.

Shaped concrete slabs ~ Shaped slabs, such as hexagons, don't easily lend themselves to curves and tend to look out of place.

Path edings

Apath edging has both an aesthetic and practical purpose. It trims the path, making it look crisply defined, structured and pleasing to the eye. Much more importantly, the edging is a structural control that stops the path from spreading under its own weight and that of people using the path. Without a good edging, the sides of the path would erode, the lawn and weeds would creep in, and the whole path would gradually spread and sag in the center.

Do paths always need edgings?

PATH EDGE OPTIONS

In general, the best edgings are made from small units that can be spaced to fit around curves. They should be chosen to blend in with the overall character of the path and its setting.

Soldier bricks

These are perfect for straight or curved, formal or informal paths in brick, stone or gravel.

Angled bricks

Angled bricks are good for a path alongside a flowerbed, to keep earth off the path.

Decorative tiles

These look good with bricks, setts and such, but terrible with natural materials like bark.

Log roll

Log-roll edging is ideal for meandering natural paths on uneven ground.

PATH EDGING EXAMPLES

Soldier bricks

Lawn flush with top of bricks

Compacted coarse sand

Bricks bedded in mortar or concrete

Compacted gravel

↗ Soldier bricks are set with the stretcher (side) face upright. This path of gravel over hardcore has the lawn flush with the top of the bricks to make mowing easy.

Wooden boards

Shallow trench filled with pea gravel to discourage weeds

Tamped concrete

Wooden strips fixed to stakes

Compacted gravel

↗ Wooden boards are fixed to stakes to edge this concrete path. The lawn is at a lower level, with a shallow, gravel-filled trench between the lawn and the boards.

Victorian tiles

Flowerbed set lower than the tiles

Compacted coarse sand

Tiles bedded in mortar or concrete

Compacted gravel

↗ These decorative tiles form an attractive edging, shown here on a path of slabs. The flowerbed is set lower than the path, so that the tile edging is on show. For best effect, use kiln-fired clay tiles rather than concrete.

PATH EDGING NOTES

Qualities of a good edging ~ All edgings need to be constructed in such a way that the path is well supported, but the definition of what constitutes a good edging changes according to the character of the path. For example, a good decorative edging would be one that is clearly on show, but a good edging for a natural path would be one that is hidden from view.

Things to avoid ~ Put decorative edgings on paths bordered by flowerbeds, rather than lawn, so that you are less likely to trip over them.

The necessity of edging ~ Some paths look best when the edge is hidden from view, like a meandering natural path made of bark, but all paths benefit from an edging. A concrete path is perhaps the only exception, and even then it needs a wooden edge during the time it is being cast.

Steps in paths

Can I have steps in my sloping garden path?

Unless your garden is as flat as a pancake, there will be places where you can include one or more steps. As well as paths, the possibilities include a sunken patio complete with steps, steps from the garden up to the patio, or from the patio down to the path. For a much grander scheme, turn the whole garden into a series of level terraces, perhaps with a patio by the house, a couple of flower borders, and steps running from one level to another.

SIMPLE STEPS IN PATHS

There are two options: dig steps into the slope of the ground, so that the sides are hidden from view, or build steps up from the slope so that the sides are on full view.

The first option is the easiest to build. The simplest steps – no more difficult than stacking children's building blocks – are those where the units that make up the steps become both the riser and the tread, as is the case when you use railroad ties.

Ties spiked together in a stack

A good tread width: 9 in

Perfect riser height: 6 in

A flight of steps made from 3 ft-long pieces of railroad tie. The 6 in thickness becomes the height of the riser.

Would it be better to have a slope than steps?

You may prefer not to have steps if some garden users are not very agile, or so that a mower, wheelbarrow or wheelchair can move unhindered. If the slope of the garden is gentle, there are other options.

Tree bark ~ A gently ascending slope of crushed tree bark is firm and dry underfoot, and easy to maintain.

Stamped concrete ~ The pattern marks in a long, sloping path of stamped concrete provide a good foothold.

STEPS IN NATURAL PATHS

Simple steps can be created by fixing logs across the width of a path and then spreading material (such as bark or gravel) behind them to make level areas, which become the treads. The logs become both the riser and the nosing to the treads. This design is very easy to build. To create a more architectural look, use railroad ties instead of logs.

Second log distanced from the first

Log held in place with stakes

Level bed of gravel

CORNER STEPS IN A PATH

When building an angled turn in a flight of steps – say where a path changes direction as it climbs up a slope – the simplest thing to do is create a "quarter dog-leg turn." In effect, this is a single square step that allows you to turn comfortably in readiness for climbing on to the next step. If the steps are 3 ft wide, the square step would measure 3 x 3 ft.

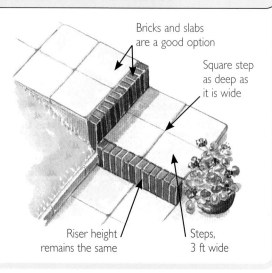

Bricks and slabs are a good option

Square step as deep as it is wide

Riser height remains the same

Steps, 3 ft wide

SAFETY CONSIDERATIONS

Seek professional advice and help if the flight of steps numbers greater than six, or if the ground is in any way unstable – such as very sandy, waterlogged, steep and rocky or steep and crumbly, or if the land has been been reclaimed.

Steps are inherently very dangerous – older people may slip on them and children may stumble and roll down them – so it is vital to do your best to make sure that they are as safe as possible. If the steps are steep, incorporate handrails. Make sure that the treads are not slippery – do not make them from materials such as polished slate or wood that is liable to get green and slimy. Always keep the riser height constant (and no more than 7 in) to avoid a situation where an unforeseen change to the rhythm of ascent or descent might catch someone unawares and cause him or her to lurch and trip.

Path solutions

The most obvious function of a garden path is as a direct walkway between two points, which takes the shortest route. A mixture of practical necessity, with a dash of decoration thrown in for good measure, successfully fulfils this garden role. Some paths are intended more as unhurried routes around the best features and views in the garden, and these may have a more decorative component to add to the enjoyment of the garden experience.

What is most important in a path?

This path circles a large country house. The border of bumpy cobbles helps persuade visitors to keep to the path.

PRACTICAL PATHS

A good, practical path has to enable you to get from A to B without getting your feet wet. It needs to be firm and dry underfoot, with no slime or puddles, and it should get you to your destination quickly. Practical paths tend to be straight, and a decent width in order to accommodate a wheelbarrow or mower. Also take into account the width of gateways when planning the path.

PRETTY PATHS

If the main purpose of a path is decorative, it is not necessary for it to follow the most direct route from A to B. It can dawdle and show off its charms, taking users on an exciting journey around the garden. See if you can create a path that visits all the garden's best features.

CONSULT THE PATH DOCTOR

AIM	SOLUTION 1	SOLUTION 2
I want to build the cheapest possible straight path from the house to the patio. It needs to be functional and solid.	Concrete is a good option for making a narrow path. Tamp the concrete to ensure that the path is rigid across its width.	Crushed wood chips are a cost-conscious option and can be obtained from most sawmills. When wood chips break down, they can be composted.
I want to build a pretty, winding path through a wooded area at the bottom of the garden. It has to travel from the garden up to the patio.	Stepping stones can look very natural – choose real stone slabs and set them in a bed of pea gravel. Allow grass to grow into the gravel.	Crushed tree bark looks good in a woodland area. Edge the path with smooth, weathered rocks or character wood such as logs and boughs.
I live by the sea and I want a path to run from the patio straight down to the water's edge. It needs to be solid and hardwearing.	Construct a pier from railroad ties. Build tracks about 2 yds apart and bridge them with the ties to make a long pier.	Collect large, weathered stone slabs and set them in a straight line like a set of giant stepping stones. Edge them with lengths of chain.
I want to have a decorative path running from the front door to the gate. It needs to be quietly decorative – subtle and traditional.	Red brick is a good option. Set the bricks in a herringbone pattern that is square with the sides of the path. Add a zigzag edging. (See page 40.)	A pea gravel path edged with zigzag bricks (see page 40) looks good in a formal setting. Spread the gravel over a base of gravel.
I have just had the roof re-tiled and I would like to use the broken tiles to make a decorative path. I want to keep costs to a minimum.	Dig a trench the width of the path and lay a layer of compacted gravel. Spread a layer of mortar and bed the tiles on edge.	Dig a trench the width of the path and edge it with brick. Pour all the tiles into the trench and break them into small, coin-sized pieces.
My garden is very boggy. I want a low-cost path that is dry and firm underfoot, and looks good in a natural setting.	Dig out a 6 in-deep trench the width of the path. Half-fill it with compacted gravel and top this with a mixture of sand and gravel followed by pea gravel.	Hammer two lines of wooden piles into the ground. Link these with rails and build a wooden pier that runs clear of the ground.

Stone steps

Stone steps look beautiful, but are they hard to build?

Steps made from real or imitation stone are time-consuming to construct, involving many stages, although no one stage is particularly tricky. If you are enthusiastic, looking for a challenge and think that you might enjoy working at a very slow, painstaking pace fitting pieces of stone together, there is no reason why you cannot build a small flight of really good-looking steps. Step-building is rather like working on an ever-changing giant jigsaw puzzle.

Steps made from salvaged flagstones. Plants have been allowed to seed themselves in the joints, giving a cottage garden feel.

REAL STONE

There are four readily available types of real stone: limestone, sandstone, slate and granite. Most garden projects are best built from either natural split sandstone or reclaimed limestone.

CUTTING STONE

As far as possible, cut stone along its grain. If, like limestone, it doesn't have a pronounced grain, use an angle grinder in conjunction with a small sledge hammer and chisel. See pages 29 and 71.

USING MORTAR

A good, smooth mortar can be made from 2 parts cement, 1 part lime and 9 parts soft sand. See page 13.

FOUNDATIONS

An average foundation is 12 in deep, with 6 in of compacted gravel and 6 in of concrete. On soft ground, make it deeper with thicker concrete. See page 16.

OPTIONS FOR STONE STEPS

Partially cut-in rustic steps in crazy paving

↘ A long flight of crazy-paving steps built up a natural slope. The steps appear to be fully cut into the slope, but in fact are partially freestanding. The sides are partly visible and banked up with large rocks. This is a good project for ground that is firm and stable.

Cut-in steps in cut stone

↘ A short flight of steps cut into the side of a terrace, with the sides of the steps built into the raised walls. This is a relatively easy project, in that the earth to the back and sides, and the walls to the sides, provide support. The front and side walls are built first, leaving a gap for the steps, and the steps are then built to fit. Slabs of York stone have been used for this project.

Freestanding steps in cut stone

↘ A beautiful flight of freestanding steps running from a courtyard up to a raised patio. The steps are relatively easy to achieve in that they are built as a solid stepped block. Rough-cut field stone is used for the sides and risers, and stone slabs for the treads. Note the attractive arch feature under the steps.

HOW TO BUILD SIMPLE STEPS

These freestanding steps provide an easy option for a natural slope, or for a low flight of three or four steps. They are made from a mixture of thin pieces of split real stone for the risers, and 18 in-square concrete pavers or slabs for the treads.

Dig out the foundation trench for the first step, making it 22 in long, 22 in wide and 12 in deep. Fill it with 6 in of compacted gravel and top with 6 in of concrete. Once the concrete has hardened, use the split stone to build a four-walled box measuring 17 in from front to back, and 16 in across, to a height of about 4 in. Fill the cavity within the box with a mixture of waste stone and concrete. Top it with mortar and bed the slabs for the treads in position.

To build the next step, repeat the procedure already described, only this time, have the top of the foundation slab level with the top of the first step.

Step 4
Dig the foundation for the second step behind the first step, repeating the procedure. The concrete should be level with the first step.

Step 3
Bed the concrete slabs for the treads on mortar, so that the leading edge overhangs the box by about an inch.

Step 2
Build a box of split stone and mortar on the foundation. Fill the box with gravel and concrete.

Step 1
Dig out the foundation for the first step. Depth of the foundation and height of the steps is set by local code.

CRAZY-PAVING STEPS

↘ These crazy-paving steps are built in much the same way as the simple steps described above – the difference is the way the stone for the crazy-paving treads is fitted. The secret of success is to spend a lot of time selecting the stone so that the corners of the steps are at right angles, and the leading edges at the front and sides of the treads (the nosings) are straight.

Center of the tread filled in with crazy stones to achieve best fit and be as level as possible

Carefully selected stones for the corners and nosings of the tread

Box to form walls of step. Built from pieces of crazy stone to best fit

Foundation of about 6 in of concrete on 6 in of compacted gravel

Wooden board to contain the concrete

MORE STONEWORK STEP DESIGNS

Much of the secret of building attractive stone steps concerns the type of stone selected for the risers. Mostly, there are two choices – you can use a stack of thin pieces of stone to make up the height of the riser, or you can use blocks that are about riser height.

It is possible to buy damaged stone from an architectural reclamation yard. Risers could be made from old limestone windowsills and suchlike, or thin pieces of old roof stone.

TROUBLESHOOTING

• Avoid using blocks of stone that need to be cut – it is much easier to use thin layers of stone.
• If the ground is unstable, dig much deeper foundations and use a greater thickness of concrete.
• Stay away from the foundations of the house and from drains.
• Always go for low risers rather than high ones – they are easier to build and safer to use.
• Avoid hard-to-cut stone such as granite.

Brick steps

Is brickwork as difficult as it looks?

If you can mix mortar and concrete, lift the weight of a brick, and lay one brick on top of another, you are capable of doing brickwork. Of course, to be successful you do have to make sure that each brick is vertically and horizontally level and square, and this requires patience, but brickwork is altogether much easier than it looks. It does not matter if your bricklaying is slightly less than perfect to start with – you will soon get better with practice.

TYPES OF BRICK

There are many types of brick; for garden projects, it is best to use well-fired (or high-fired) house bricks, or engineering bricks. These are harder than ordinary bricks, waterproof and frostproof. Low-fired interior-grade bricks are not suitable.

DESIGNING BRICK STEPS

In order to produce good brickwork, the challenge is to create a design that is mostly comprised of whole bricks (minimizing the need to cut bricks), in which the horizontal courses or layers are well bonded or interlocked, and the bricks are arranged so that the vertical joints in neighboring courses are staggered.

FOUNDATIONS

The bottom step in a flight always needs a solid foundation of concrete on compacted gravel. Subsequent steps only need gravel, equal in depth to the height of the riser.

CUTTING BRICK

Usually, bricks are cut in half across their length to produce two half-bricks or brickbats; sometimes, however, they are halved along their width. To cut a brick, mark a guideline with chalk, position the brick on the lawn or a piece of old carpet, set a brick chisel on the guideline, and give it a single blow with a small sledge hammer.

USING MORTAR

Mortar should be smooth, without being too wet. When working with mortar, use the large builder's trowel to scoop it up, set it down, and to slice off the excess mortar; use the small pointing trowel to fill joints and rake out mortar to expose the edges of the bricks.

LAYING BRICKS AND KEEPING THEM LEVEL, STRAIGHT AND EVENLY SPACED

Set the brick on a bed of mortar, tapping it into place with the handle of the trowel, then "butter" the end with mortar. Repeat with the next brick in line. Every other brick or so, take a reading with the carpenter's level and make adjustments so that the bricks are aligned with each other and are both vertically and horizontally level. For beginners, it is good practice to use a small torpedo level to test each brick as it is being laid. Some beginners prefer to do the tapping process with a rubber hammer.

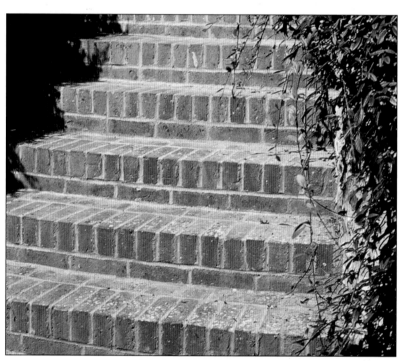

A beautiful flight of traditional cut-in brick steps leading from a courtyard up to a raised patio. Note the way the bricks are arranged on the leading edge of the treads so that each step curves out in a gentle convex arc.

A single step from a path to a patio, with the edge of the patio becoming the step. Note how the bricks are set upright to make a soldier course.

OPTIONS FOR BRICK STEPS

↗ *A very basic, easy-to-build flight of steps running from a sunken patio up to a lawn.*

↗ *A flight of curved steps that reflects the shape of the large, circular brick and sett patio.*

↗ *A simple brick step, linking two non-brick patio areas, provides an eye-catching detail.*

↗ *A basic flight of steps. The bottom step is flush with the surface of the patio.*

HOW TO BUILD BASIC BRICKWORK STEPS

Steps for soft ground
with soldier bricks forming the tread

→ This classic two-step flight of brickwork steps, with concrete over gravel under every tread, is a good option for soft ground. The slab of concrete under every step compensates for damp clay soil.

In the project illustrated, the steps link two patios, one of which is raised slightly above the other. In this instance, there are actually three steps, with the bottom step being inset and flush with the surface of the lower patio. If you have a damp site and you want to make absolutely sure that your steps are going to stay put, with little or no movement, this is a good design to go for.

Tread nosing of soldier bricks backed by a stretcher course

All bricks are of a high-fired exterior grade

Bottom tread set flush with the surface of the lower patio

Drain behind the bottom step

6 in of concrete on 6 in of compacted gravel (under every step)

Steps for a courtyard corner
with non-slip treads

Step 4
Decide how deep you want the tread to be (about the length of a brick is good) and then build another three courses of bricks.

Step 3
Fill the front 12 in of the box with concrete and use a thin stick to create a pattern on the surface. Fill the back with gravel and construction rubble to save on the cost of concrete.

Step 2
Build up three courses of stretcher bond (stretcher faces on show – see illustration), so that you have a four-sided rectangular box that runs back to the wall.

↙ These steps are designed to run from the corner of a courtyard to a raised patio area, and are supported at the back and on one side.

Step 5
Continue building the other steps, with the top surface of each step tamped with a pattern to make a non-slip surface.

Step 1
Dig out the whole step area to a depth of 12 in and lay 6 in of compacted gravel. Top with 6 in of concrete.

Wooden steps

I enjoy working in wood: how do I make steps?

Wooden steps are great, both for a country cottage garden or a small city patch. The level of skill required to make them depends upon the design: step construction does not have to involve complicated woodwork. For example, railroad tie steps are heavy work, but technically they are very easy to do. The steps to raised decking (shown below center) are very straightforward because they use screws, nuts and bolts, rather than complex joints.

This flight of steps uses full-length ties for the treads, quarter-ties for the stub (support) posts, and an infill of crushed stone.

A flight of steps running up to an area of raised decking – a simple construction with all joints either bolted or screwed.

This long flight of steps consists of pressure-treated logs for the treads, with an infill of crushed stone.

STEPS FOR RAISED DECKING

➔ The secret of these steps – the factor that makes them easy – is that all the joints are achieved by sawing off-the-shelf sections of wood to length, setting one piece of wood against another, and fixing them with a couple of screws or a nut, washer and bolt.

Banister rail

Stair treads screwed to step bearers

Support bolted to the post to hold the stringer (side joist)

Post set in a hole with gravel and concrete

Vertical balusters screwed to rails

Step bearers screwed to a stringer (side joist)

MORE WOODEN STEPS

If you like the idea of wooden steps, but find the idea of making them a bit scary, you can buy a stair kit.

However, for the most part, the easiest way to build a flight of wooden steps – with up to four treads – is to use lengths of railroad ties. Ties are about 6 in thick and 8 in wide and make ideal steps, the thickness forming the riser height. Many suppliers are happy to cut ties to suit. The most economical option is to design steps that use ties without creating any waste: for example, a 3 yd-long tie can be divided to make three 1 yd-long steps.

Quick wooden steps

See page 45 for the quickest ways to make a flight of steps.

Natural steps

The aim of a set of natural steps is to create something that looks as if it has evolved naturally as part of the landscape – like a group of stones that makes a platform to a higher level, or fallen logs stretched across a gentle slope, behind which debris has accumulated to provide a natural step. It could be a tangle of roots that provides a foothold, or soil erosion on a slope that has formed a convenient place to move up from.

What are natural steps?

This flight of steps was designed to blend into the rock garden and become a part of it. Plants assist by tumbling over the borders.

STEPS THAT BLEND IN

To blend in with nature, the steps must be made from materials such as wood or stone, and be put together in such a way that they fool you into believing that they are natural – like slabs of stone stacked on top of each other, or crushed tree bark piled behind a log, or terraces of gravel or crushed rock. Try to harmonize with the site and pick materials appropriate to the natural appearance of the area or the theme you are creating – use wood for a forest-type area, boulders and stone for a hillside, washed stone for a coast, or salvaged material for a 'back to nature' inner-city site.

OPTIONS

Steps made from tree bark and logs look good in a forest-type garden, while a scree of crushed stone looks great in a hillside garden. If you live in an area that has an industrial past, you may like to consider a look that suggests that nature is taking over, by incorporating rusty iron and wooden beams.

HOW TO BUILD ROCK STEPS

The ideal would be to use massive weathered stones for each step, but such stones are usually too expensive to buy and too heavy to lift. An easier option is to make each step from two or three slabs of stone mortared together.

→ Set out the shape of the first step and dig a 12 in-deep hole for the foundation. Fill it with 6 in of compacted gravel topped with 6 in of concrete. Take the first stone slab and bed it in mortar. Mortar the second stone on top of the first. When the first step is finished, dig away the ground behind it and pack it with gravel as the foundation for the next step. Continue as previously described.

Smaller rocks in and around the arrangement

Two smaller slabs bedded in mortar to make the second step

Gravel packed behind the first step

12 in-deep hole; 6 in of concrete on 6 in of compacted gravel

Three large slabs mortared together to look like a weathered stone

Decorative steps

There are hundreds of ways to create steps that are a little out of the ordinary. Steps can be decorative in the sense that they have a sculpted form or shape, with curved treads or ornate rails; they can have color applied to the surface with paint or mosaics; they can be enhanced with applied carved reliefs, such as Victorian terracotta tiles; or the materials themselves can contribute an exciting decorative effect in stone, metal, wood or brick.

OPTIONS FOR DECORATIVE STEPS

Although the choice is huge, you do have to choose something to fit in with your home and garden. For example, terracotta tiles look good in a traditional country cottage garden, decorative woodwork goes nicely with decking, mosaics of broken tiles or crockery, applied to flat surfaces, can look wonderful in a small courtyard setting, and so on. Look at your garden and home, and consider your skills and how much time you want to spend. It is best to avoid fashion statements that are likely to date.

Brick and flagstone curves

↗ *A stepped edge to a raised patio, with brick risers and flagstone treads.*

Blue decking

↗ *Wooden steps, leading up to a forest patio, are given a blue-gray color wash for an aged effect.*

Red brick and crazy paving

↗ *A traditional mix: brick for the tread nosings and crazy paving for the infill.*

Blue and white

↗ *White steps with blue treads, cross-braced rails and turned post finials.*

Diamond lattice trellis

↗ *Steps leading up to a raised island patio, with lattice trellis at the sides.*

Fretted and painted pink

↗ *Decking steps with fretted and pierced details, painted a delicate pink to match the cottage.*

Country cottage green

↗ *A relaxed look – trellis with green-painted risers.*

STYLE NOTES

When you build steps, they will be as much an expression of your taste as any other feature in your house or garden, so the design deserves careful consideration. But remember that unlike rooms in your home that can be restyled fairly easily to suit changing fads and fashions, it is more difficult to rebuild steps and so the most successful garden styles tend to be traditional, classic and timeless.

PRACTICALITIES

As with any steps, it is most important that decorative steps are safe. However you choose to adorn them, the decoration must not pose a hazard.

So if, for example, you were thinking about decorating the steps with glazed tiles or shells, they should be kept to the sides and the risers, and not applied to the treads, because these must have a level, non-slip surface. Always make safety a priority.

Building tips

The decoration has to survive extremes of weather – sun, wind and rain.

Brick ~ Use high-fired water- and frost-resistant bricks. (See page 58.)

Stone ~ Lay stone with the run of the grain on one of the edge faces, rather than uppermost, so that it doesn't collect water. (See page 56.)

Paint and finishes ~ Use paints, varnishes and finishes that are designed for outdoor use.

Ceramic tiles ~ Use high-fired quarry tiles for large areas. If you want to incorporate areas of mosaic made of broken bathroom tiles or crockery, use waterproof cement and grout.

Doorsteps

Adoorstep undoubtedly needs to be fit for its purpose – to get you from one level to another – but its secondary function (some would say most important function) is to form a visual introduction to the house. The doorstep (consisting of one or more steps) needs to be attractive and welcoming, and can also convey more subtle messages, for example the design might declare that you have good taste, or the large size hint that you are generous.

DOORSTEP OPTIONS

↗ A single step with a porch over it and seats to the side makes a grand entrance.

↗ Two flights of crazy-paving stone steps leading up a gentle slope, with a short linking path.

↗ A generous pair of decking steps built over a single existing high brick step.

↗ A semicircular step built from half-bricks and half of a patio circle tile-and-slab kit.

STYLE

Doorsteps are quite a challenge: they must get you comfortably from one level to another, look sufficiently grand and welcoming, and they also have to draw your eye up to the door. It is best to choose a design with a low riser height – no more than 6 in – and the broadest possible width.

IMPORTANT NOTES

Doorsteps have three important elements – riser height, tread depth and step width. You need to get them all right.

Riser height ~ A good, comfortable, easy-to-use doorstep has risers that are no lower than 4 in and no higher than 6 in, with all the risers in the flight of steps the same height.

Tread depth ~ The tread depth (the distance from the tread nosing, or edge, back to the face of the next riser) must be made up from one or more foot-lengths – no shorter than 9 in and as long as you like.

Step width ~ The step needs to be at least as wide as the doorway – say about 30 in – but the wider the better. One good option is to have the steps fanning out from the doorway in a series of ever-widening curves.

HOW TO BUILD A BRICK DOORSTEP

↘ This traditional doorstep is made from old, high-fired bricks. The riser height is equal to half a brick (about 4 ½ in). Lay a 6 in-thick concrete foundation slab for the bottom step. Set the bottom row of soldier bricks in place to make the first riser, half-fill the resultant cavity with concrete, and lay the bricks that make the bottom tread. Build the second riser, and continue up the flight. When you get to paving the top step, the bricks are laid in a stretcher bond for the straight bit, and a herringbone for the quarter-circle.

Tread infill made from bricks laid on edge

Stretcher bond for the straight area

A herringbone pattern to fill the quarter-circle

Bricks on edge fanned round the curve

Riser made from a row of soldier bricks

Concrete laid to half the depth of the bottom soldier bricks

Concrete pavers on the existing path

Patio furniture

Patio furniture needs to be attractive, inviting, well built, designed for the job, and above all comfortable. Furnish your patio with the same care as a room in your home. Don't rush into making a purchase – instead, wait until you are sure of your requirements and then shop around.

A combined bench and table is especially useful if you plan to eat out in the garden with the children.

SUITABILITY

Think about how you plan to use the patio, and decide what type of furniture you need to fulfil these needs. Are you just going to sit on the patio for the occasional half hour to read a newspaper, in which case a bench or chairs would be suitable, or do you intend to sunbathe, in which case a lounger would be more appropriate. If you would like to eat outdoors, do you need a small occasional table for snacks, a larger, family-size combined bench and table, or something more elegant for entertaining?

➔ *A "steamer" chair is both attractive and comfortable, offering the opportunity to lounge in style.*

↗ *This easy-to-move wheeled bench has an integral table, making it doubly useful.*

Requirements	Options
Dining We want a table big enough for the family. It must be strong, with an easy-wipe surface so that I don't have to worry about spills. It must suit a country garden.	There are lots of options, such as plastic tables with separate chairs, or metal dining suites, but the best option for a family is a wooden table. Spills do not matter – you just scrub it down with soap and water.
Reclining I want a really comfortable recliner. It must be strong, but light enough for me to move on my own. It has got to be modern and appropriate for a design-conscious city garden.	Wooden recliners look good, and metal recliners are relatively inexpensive, but you cannot do better than some of the large plastic recliners – they are light, attractive and amazingly comfortable.
Style is important We are seeking some really stylish furniture, because we do a lot of entertaining and need to impress clients. We have a large garden with lots of designer features. Money no object.	If you want something extra-special, and are not worried about the cost, you could contact an architect or designer who specializes in one-off designs, and maybe have something built in marble or stainless steel.
Mostly ornamental We want furniture to blend in with our traditional Victorian house. We like lots of ornamental details and want to leave the furniture out in the garden as a permanent feature.	The best solution is to buy some genuine or reproduction Victorian cast-iron furniture. Some architectural reclamation yards specialize in Victorian pieces. Avoid anything that looks cracked.
Stacking, folding or knock-down We are looking for furniture for our very small town garden. We will need to put it away for the winter, in a small shed and a loft space over the garage, so it must be lightweight.	There are many easy-to-store options, but they often compromise on comfort. One traditional fold-up design, back in fashion, is the deckchair with canvas seat. It is both comfortable and easy to store.

MATERIALS AND STYLES

Victorian reproduction

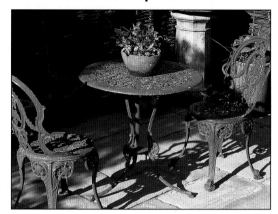

Patio furniture comes in a huge choice of materials and styles – wood, metal, plastic, modern, traditional, high-tech and so on. When deciding what to buy, take into account the style of your garden. A modern, minimalist city yard might be best served by contemporary metalwork or plastic, or design classics. More traditional country and cottage-style gardens would welcome wooden furniture – choose from classic hardwood designs, rustic concoctions or folk-style shapes. Stonework also blends well into traditional gardens, and can be used to create permanent, weatherproof benches. These look striking, but are not the most comfortable option to choose.

← *Reproduction Victorian cast-iron furniture, made of aluminum, looks stylish and is much lighter than the original.*

Folding, rigid and reclining

↗ *Three chair options. A slanted back is more comfortable than an upright one.*

↗ *A wooden "steamer" recliner harmonizes perfectly with a decking patio.*

Rustic

↗ *Rustic furniture looks good in a country garden. You will need cushions for comfort.*

Classical

↗ *Stone is good if you value classic longevity over comfort.*

Design classic

↗ *Look for designer chairs at garage sales.*

Teak

↗ *Teak is long-lasting. Buy it from a reputable sustainable source.*

Folk

↗ *Folk-style chairs can be made cheaply from salvaged wood.*

QUICK AND EASY FURNITURE SOLUTIONS

Instant furniture can be made from planks and concrete blocks: just stack the blocks and lay planks across them to make tables and benches. Seats from classic cars make inexpensive, comfortable, arty furniture. Traditional seaside deckchairs are reasonably cheap, and are available in strong colors and patterns that will jazz up any patio.

THINGS TO AVOID

Avoid furniture that relies on springs and elastic, because it is not durable. Stainless-steel patio furniture may have weak bolts, and if one of these shears off, it renders the item useless. Make sure you only buy items that are weatherproof and can be safely left outside, unless you are prepared to dash out when rain threatens and bring them indoors.

Safety

Fold-up chairs are a bad idea if children and older people will be using them, especially if the clips and locks are fragile. Such chairs have a nasty habit of folding up and nipping fingers.

Some plastics eventually become brittle and render chairs liable to collapse if you lean back on them.

WINTER STORAGE

Apart from furniture that is built in situ, or made from heavy oak, most pieces need to be stored for the winter. Even plastic quickly degrades when it is left out in all weathers. Think about where you are going to put it before purchasing.

MAINTENANCE

At the end of the season, wooden furniture needs to be protected with paint, teak oil or creosote. Traditionally, gardeners used to brush large benches and chairs with creosote and set them upside down in a shed. Modern plastic and metal chairs are best wiped over with a damp cloth and stored in a dry place. Soft cushions should be stored in plastic bags and kept inside the house, in dry and warm conditions, away from possible colonization by mice. Use a small paintbrush to dab springs and bolts with a light oil, to stop rust.

Furniture you can make

I enjoy easy DIY – could I make patio furniture?

There is a long tradition of householders making garden furniture (such as porch chairs, swings, picnic benches and, of course, patio furniture) from whatever was at hand. In the United States, old crates were used to make Adirondack chairs, in Germany and Switzerland furniture was constructed from rough-sawn timber, and in England rustic chairs were fashioned from fruit tree wood. Enthusiasm is more important than technical ability: there is a project for everyone.

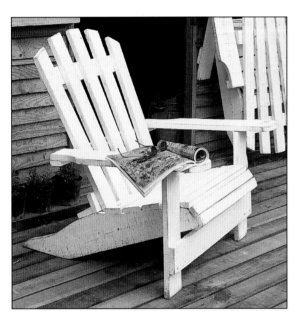

IS IT WORTH MAKING MY OWN GARDEN FURNITURE?

Making your own garden furniture is very worthwhile – it can be done for almost no cost, the results are long-lasting and stylish, and the whole activity is very enjoyable. There is nothing quite so satisfying as sitting in a chair you have made and listening to friends admire your handiwork. There are projects suitable for all abilities – you can try anything from a very basic, straightforward piece such as a built-in bench, to something more involved, such as an Adirondack chair. All can be made using a minimum of tools and equipment.

INSPIRATIONS

← *A classic example of an Adirondack chair, made from old crates fixed with screws.*

Visit a museum and look at farmhouse and folk furniture of the past (such as three-legged stools, board tables and plank-back chairs) to get inspiration, and then have a go. Limit yourself to using simple hand tools and basic hammer and nail joints.

THE POSSIBILITIES

PERMANENT (BUILT-IN) FURNITURE

- Tables and benches can be made from stacks of concrete blocks topped with heavy planks or railroad ties.

- Chairs and benches can be built entirely from bricks.

- A bench can be made from two sections cut from a telephone pole (these make the two supports) bridged with a plank.

- Low walls always attract people to sit on them – consider building special walls of just the right height.

MOVABLE FURNITURE

- Chairs and benches can be made from willow wands nailed together. Start with a simple stool form – a plank seat and four legs – and then try adding arms and a backrest.

- A low stool can be made from a section cut from a tree. If you want to move it, you tip it over and roll it.

- A heavy bench can be manoeuvred with ease if you give it a pair of wheels and a handle, rather like a long wheelbarrow.

- A traditional wooden picnic table is light enough to move easily. If you want to follow the sun or shade, you simply lift or drag it to a new location.

WOOD

- Railroad ties make good benches. Make sure you avoid those that are oozing oil and tar.

- The wood from old fruit trees is good for making rustic furniture – the wood is scented and an exciting shape.

- Thin willow wands can be woven into screens or chair backs.

- Wood that has been pressure-treated with preservative is not suitable for tabletops that will hold food, unless varnished.

STONE

- Benches can be built using cut stone topped with planks.

- Small stone cairns (small pillars built with field stone and mortar) make good stools and table legs.

METAL

- Tables, chairs and benches can be built using exhibition-grade aluminum scaffolding, with scaffolding clips for joints.

- Old tractor seats make attractive and stylish stools.

Important dimensions

There are certain standard dimensions for furniture (measure manufactured pieces in your home), but you might have to make changes to suit your needs. For example, a standard upright chair is usually from 16 in to 18 in high, but if you are above or below average height, or are making an easy chair, you will have to make adjustments.

Make a mock-up

To test out dimensions, make a mock-up – use a box for a chair, and a pile of bricks for a table. Make a series of gradual adjustments to the mock-up until it feels correct and comfortable.

29 in

7 in

16 3/4 in

HOW TO BUILD A STONE TABLE

The pillar is made of thin, random pieces of stone such as reclaimed roof stone (split limestone) or field stone, and three slabs about 3 in thick. The base slab and capital slab can be any type of flagstone; for the tabletop you may prefer to use a slate or limestone flagstone, which has more character.

Step 5
Trowel mortar over the capital slab, then take the tabletop slab and bed it level.

Step 4
Trowel mortar over the top of the pillar, then take the capital slab and bed it level.

Step 6
With the point of a trowel, rake some mortar out of the joints in the pillar, so the edges of the stone are revealed.

Step 3
When building the pillar, do your best to keep vertical joints staggered.

Step 2
Build a pillar from thin stone and mortar, making it about 30 in high and about 20 in diameter. Check that each course is level.

Step 1
Find a base slab and set it level on the patio (or flush with the surface of the lawn).

HOW TO MAKE WOODEN SEATING

This corner bench is made from standard off-the-shelf sections of rough-sawn wood directly from the sawmill. The seat is supported by four side leg frames, and one corner leg frame, each consisting of two legs joined at the top by a stretcher or linking bar (two for the corner frame). Seat boards are fixed to the leg frames, and the front edges of the seat are finished with fascia strips. The whole structure is fixed with two stainless-steel screws at each joint, and finished with water-based, exterior-grade paint. The attractive herringbone miter joint where the two halves of the bench meet is created by butting the seat boards end to side, and then side to end, with each successive strip.

Step 5
Cut four boards to length for the fascias. Screw them to the edges of the seat boards.

Fascia

Corner leg frame

Stretcher

Side leg frame

Step 4
Screw the seat boards to the leg frames. Working from the outer board, each subsequent board is the width of a board less in length than the previous one. A herringbone effect is created where the boards meet at the corner.

Step 1
For each of the four side leg frames, cut two legs from 4x4s about 16 in long and a stretcher from a 2x4 to the length of four of the boards to be used for the set. Fix together with two screws at each joint.

Step 2
For the corner leg frame, cut the legs the same as the side frame but the stretcher slightly longer since it is a diagonal.

Step 3
Position the outer two leg frames so they are aligned and square with each other and the corner frame is at a 45-degree angle to both sides.

Planting for patios

Patios are usually designed to be sheltered and warm, and are often a contrasting environment to the rest of the garden. There are three key things to remember when selecting plants for patio containers: choose varieties suitable for a container in the allocated position, whether sunny or shady, water regularly and feed periodically according to the plant's requirements. Pots, troughs, raised beds and hanging baskets can all play a part.

Planting options

Containers ~ A container can be anything from a ceramic pot to an old watering can. Just add a drainage hole at the bottom if there isn't one.

Planters ~ Planters are larger and heavier versions of containers, for example a lead tank or an old sink.

Trellis or pergola ~ Good for supporting climbing plants and can also be used as a screen (see page 70).

Planting pockets ~ You can leave slabs or bricks out of the patio surface to make pockets for small plants.

An old stone sink propped up on bricks, and a large ceramic pot, make perfect partners on a traditional brick patio.

HOW TO GET STARTED

Study your patio and then make a list to describe the conditions (such as dry or shady), the role you want the plants to play, and the way you wish to display the plants.

For example, let's say that your patio is very sunny, you want to have climbing plants all around to give shade and privacy, and you want the plants to be displayed in large ceramic pots. The climbers will have to be mainly evergreen to provide a screen, and tolerant of sun and dry conditions. Certain varieties of clematis, jasmine and honeysuckle might be suitable.

CONTAINER OPTIONS

If we define a container as being smaller than a planter – so it can be moved with relative ease – it can consist of anything from a large tin can to a chimney pot. There are many exciting options. You could make a collection of galvanized buckets, watering cans or old saucepans. Anything that is free from sharp edges, and large enough to house your patio plants, is suitable. A group of ceramic pots, in the same color, will make a visual impact and provide the patio with a consistent theme.

An old galvanized bucket is an attractive container for small plants.

Pots are an easy option and good when you want to group plants.

Hanging baskets look good cascading from a pergola over the patio.

Unattractive plastic pots can be disguised in a secondary container such as an old galvanized bath.

Old-fashioned chimney pots make striking display stands, perfect for a special planting feature.

PLANTER OPTIONS

Planters are much the same as containers, only bigger – once they are in place and bulging with plants, they are pretty much immovable. The point here is that unlike containers that can easily be moved to suit your whims, a planter is usually installed and then left alone. In other words, planters require a lot of forward planning – the shape, the size, the position and, of course, the way the plants within the planter are going to be selected and grouped – so that you do not make mistakes.

A dwarf evergreen in a picket box.

A planter made from a reconstituted stone kit. The blocks all fit together like a puzzle and are bonded with mortar or resin.

A long picket trough concealing plastic pots – useful if you want an ever-changing display.

A wooden trough with an integral trellis.

A stone sink mounted on a length of tie.

PLANTING POCKETS

A few bricks have been omitted from this patio to provide a planting pocket that has been filled with low, creeping plants.

This delightful feature, incorporated into a stone wall, is the perfect home for a slow-growing, drooping variety.

HOW TO MAKE A STONE RAISED BED

Permanent raised beds are a great option for an existing stone or brick patio. They can be built using easily obtainable materials such as bricks or concrete blocks, positioned precisely where you want them and, best of all, built to a height and size to suit your specific needs. The only proviso is that the patio must be well built, with a strong foundation of compacted hardcore. For ease, design a rectilinear or square bed (so that it can be made from whole bricks as much as possible) to fit within the grid of your patio.

Step 3
Build the walls with bricks and mortar, staggering the joints in the courses. Rake mortar out of a vertical joint at the bottom of the bed for drainage. Spread a generous layer of mortar on the top course; bed the coping slabs in place.

Step 4
Put loose rubble in the bottom of the bed to promote free drainage. Fill the bed with a mixture of topsoil and peat, and plant your chosen plants.

Step 2
Design the bed so that the sides are built of whole bricks as much as possible. Lay the courses of bricks (dry) to see how the bed will look.

Step 1
Make sure that the patio is well built, with a foundation of concrete or compacted gravel. If you are not sure, lift the paving to check.

Container and tub planting guide

A patio is the perfect place for feature containers, planters and raised beds. Perhaps you need climbing plants to tumble and cascade from an overhead pergola, or you want to be surrounded by whispering grasses. Maybe you like the idea of sitting amidst a jungle of old-fashioned cottage garden plants. The listings below will give you a few ideas to get you started.

Favorite flowers	Good foliage	Just bulbs	Good combinations
Snapdragon *Antirrhinum majus* A short-lived perennial providing lots of color. Dwarf varieties look good in grouped containers. Prefers full sun.	**Plantain lily** *Hosta* 'Ginko Craig' Leaves with white margins and lots of compact, bell-shaped flowers.	**Golden garlic** *Allium moly* Bright yellow flowers. Likes a rocky soil and lots of sun.	**Bright summer color** Flame creeper and Chinese Virginia creeper *Tropaeoleum speciosum; Parthenocissus henryana* Flame creeper has bright red flowers; Chinese Virginia creeper has green or bronze leaves. An exotic mix of climbers, perfect for a pergola.
Pimpernel *Anagallis monellii* Beautiful blue flowers with pink centers. A dwarf bushy tender perennial, which flowers from summer until autumn.	**Red-hot poker** *Kniphofia* 'Little Maid' Grass-like leaves and pale yellow flowers.	**Daffodil** *Narcissus* Many shades available; looks good in clumps.	**Cottage plants** Pansy and stonecrop *Viola* 'Molly Sanderson'; *Sedum kamtschaticum* The intense purple flowers of the pansies and the golden-orange flowers of the stonecrop make a stunning combination for a low border.
Double daisy *Bellis perennis* A mass of very pretty pom-pom flowers in red, pink or white. Likes sun or partial shade.	**Dead nettle** *Lamium maculatum* Nettle-like leaves; various leaf colors.	**Windflower** *Anemone blanda* Blue flowers. Likes sun and well-drained soil.	**Climbers** Honeysuckle and climbing snapdragon *Lonicera periclymenum; Asarina antirrhinifolia* The exotic flowers of the honeysuckle look great with the violet flowers of the snapdragon.
Busy Lizzie *Impatiens* cultivars Lots of red, pink, white or orange flowers. Likes a rich soil. Thrives in sun or partial shade.	**Cobweb houseleek** *Sempervivum arachnoideum* Decorative leaf rosettes. **Creeping Jenny** *Lysimachia nummularia* 'Aurea' Striking golden leaves.	**Indian shot plant** *Canna* hybrids Tall, exotic and showy. Needs sun. **Snake's head fritillary** *Fritillaria meleagris* White, purple and pink flowers in spring.	**Just grasses** Blue fescue and Chinese fountain grass *Festuca glauca; Pennisetum alopecuroides* Blue fescue looks stunning alongside the tall rust-brown plumes of the fountain grass.

Pergolas and trellises

Are attractive pergolas and trellises hard to build?

Atrellis is not a very sophisticated object – just a number of thin, rough-sawn battens fixed together with nails – but when it is in place and covered with climbing plants, it can totally transform a patio. Much the same goes for a pergola, which is just a collection of beams, and yet can become a real feature. Pergolas are easy to build, because the construction is just basic woodwork. Trellises are readily available at garden centers, but also simple to make yourself.

PERGOLAS

A pergola can turn a patio into an exciting living area, which is more of a sophisticated room than a paved area. It makes the patio feel more defined and solid. Once a pergola is draped in plants, it becomes a beautiful, shady retreat – a true green room.

Pergola options

A corner pergola with integral screen and seat

An open pergola – just a plant support

A roof designed to give maximum shade

A porch-type pergola with lattice screens

A simple design made with rustic poles

A design to match the style of the house

How to make a pergola

A pergola is made up from four elements: main posts, beams that link the posts, rafters that sit on the beams, and battens that top the lot.

Beam and rafter shapes

Cyma curve

Classic round nose

Simple angle

Modern round nose

Concave curve

Quarter round

A simple pergola structure

Step 3
Bridge the beams with rafters set at right angles

Step 4
Bridge the rafters with a roof of battens.

Step 2
Bridge the posts with beams. Fix the joints with metal straps or patent fixings.

Step 1
Set the main posts in holes deep enough for local code; top up each hole with concrete.

TRELLISES

At one level, a trellis is no more than a frame designed to support a climbing plant, but it can also be a highly patterned, eye-catching feature, which is more an architectural statement than a mere support for plants.

Trellis types range from a very simple, shop-bought lattice of slats that you screw directly to the wall of your house, to a free-standing screen complete with an arched top, one or more doorways, and posts with carved finials. However, it is also easy to make your own trellis, using low-cost materials and the simplest of hand tools – a saw, drill and a hammer. If you would like to enhance your patio with a stunning decorative feature, now is your chance.

↗ *A trellis designed to be used as a backdrop for a special sculpture.*

↗ *A portable hinged and folding trellis screen.*

↗ *A folding trellis designed as a corner feature.*

Good plants for a pergola or trellis

The essence of a successful pergola or trellis is of course the plants that clothe it and embellish the wooden structure. The following plants are all climbers, which draw the eye upwards.

Evergreen with feature leaves
Canary Island ivy (*Hedera canariensis*): glossy leaves, red stems
Persian ivy (*Hedera colchica*): large, heart-shaped leaves
Common ivy (*Hedera helix*): various colors, self-clinging

Perennial with feature flowers or fruit
Golden hop (*Humulus lupulus* 'Aureus'): gold leaves, hop flowers
Italian honeysuckle (*Lonicera caprifolium*): orange berries
Snail flower (*Phaseolus caracalla*): orange-yellow flowers, beans

Perennial and annual with scented flowers
Clematis – early (*Clematis montana* f. *grandiflora*): white flowers
Clematis – late (*Clematis tangutica*): yellow, bell-like flowers
Cup and saucer vine (*Cobaea scandens*): cream to purple flowers

Note: common names and varieties vary from country to country

Walls and dividers

Building a wall might look like a difficult job, but is in fact a series of small, easy tasks. Most brick walls are built with the stretcher or header face of the brick on view. Each row is called a course, and the wall is usually topped with a coping. The pattern bricks are laid in is termed the bond. The object of the bond is to stagger the vertical joints in order to create a strong wall. A simple stretcher bond can be used to create either a single- or double-brick wall.

I have never built a wall: is it difficult?

STONE WALLS

Stone walls are usually built up from thin, flat pieces of stone bedded in mortar. If it is necessary to cut stone, use found pieces of a type that splits down into easy-to-use, square-faced pieces. Support the stone on a piece of old carpet, and use a small sledge hammer with a brick chisel for general cutting, or a cold chisel for more delicate cutting.

If existing brick or stone walls are in a poor condition, there are ways to brighten them up. The quickest solution is to paint the whole area. You could plant climbers (against trellis panels fixed to the walls if you wish). If you want a thorough renovation of the walls, rent a sand blaster to clean back the surface, and then make good-quality repairs.

→ *This impressive patio water feature has been built without changing the underlying structure of the patio or the wall – no digging or construction work. The plant has transformed the wall.*

↗ *A country garden wall made from cut stone, old bricks and tiles.*

↗ *A retaining wall with a coping top and an integral bench seat, made from reconstituted stone blocks.*

QUICK IDEAS FOR DIVIDING UP YOUR PATIO AREA

Folding screens ~ A three-part trellis screen can be opened out and repositioned to suit the changing position of the sun and the direction of the wind.

Hanging plants ~ Basket plants can be hung from a pergola to create a fast-growing screen of cascading foliage.

Curtains ~ An area can be curtained off with one of the modern pavilion tents, or best of all with a traditional striped canvas awning, providing shade and privacy.

HOW TO BUILD A WALL IN BRICK OR STONE

Brick and stone garden walls need a solid foundation. As a general guide, the concrete foundation slab must be two to three times the width of the proposed wall. (Err on the side of caution and make a thicker, wider slab if you are uncertain.) Dry-stone walls are made of carefully stacked stones and do not use mortar. See also pages 32–33, 48–49, 58–59 (brick); 26–27, 28–29, 56–57 (stone).

Safety notes

If a brick or stone garden wall is to be more than chest height, you must dig a deeper trench – say 16 in deep – and increase the thickness of the concrete slab to 8–10 in.

Freestanding brick wall, one brick thick

Step 4
Use a trowel to rake out excess mortar and to tool it to an angled finish.

Step 3
Use a carpenter's level to check that every brick is vertically plumb and horizontally level.

Step 2
Lay the courses of bricks with mortar, staggering the vertical joints.

Step 1
Dig a trench 12 in deep and 12 in wide. Fill with 4 in of compacted gravel and 4 in of concrete.

Freestanding wall made of field stone

Step 4
Select stones with one straight face, and place them on top of the wall with this face outermost.

Step 3
Lay the stone with staggered vertical joints and long "tie" stones running through the thickness of the wall.

Step 2
Fill the trench with 4 in of compacted gravel followed by 8 in of concrete.

Step 1
Dig a trench 16 in deep and three times the width of the wall.

Ornaments and decoration

I love ornamentation – what can you suggest?

A patio is a place that you can decorate and embellish to your heart's content – it can be anything you want it to be. Treat your patio as a blank canvas, and let rip and enjoy yourself. Perhaps you are inspired by Victoriana, stark minimalism, Celtic art, American folk art or all things gold: the possibilities for interesting decorative effects are numerous. You can even treat the area as an exhibition space, and change the display theme frequently.

Birds will love this reconstituted stone cat! Sculptures of animals are a perennial favorite for the garden.

PLANNING YOUR LOOK

The bottom line about designing a patio space complete with ornaments and decoration is that in order to realize your vision, you have to plan methodically – even if you want it to be a shrine to anarchic chaos. For example, if you want the patio to be covered with decorative mosaics, you will need to provide surfaces to create them on. If you want to display a collection of bonsai, you will need lots of small niches. A statue might be displayed to best effect by building a small plinth.

Sculpture

A traditional brick and stone patio is the perfect place to display sculpture, such as ceramic figures, ironwork, cast concrete busts or three-dimensional mosaics. Consider how you want the sculpture to be viewed and then shape the space accordingly, with blank walls and niches.

TOPIARY

If you want topiary as a patio feature, don't lose sight of the fact that it is a living plant. Not only does it need sunlight, watering, and just the right soil conditions, it will also increase in size. You must take these factors into account when including topiary in your design.

IDEAS AND GUIDELINES FOR PATIO ORNAMENTS AND DECORATION

Mosaics

Mosaics can be embedded into walls and floors, or used as surface decoration for structures such as brick-built benches and tables. Use either traditional glass tiles, ceramic tiles, or even items such as pebbles, shells or broken crockery.

Wall features

Patio walls provide the perfect display space for weatherproof items that you have collected on your travels, such as ethnic masks or carved reliefs.

Pots

Pots are uniquely exciting in that they are both decorative and hold plants. Consider setting them at various levels to create a cascade of color.

Bird bath

An attractive bird bath will entice birds and give you plenty of activity to watch as they enjoy splashing about. Place it so that you can view it from your favorite patio chair, or perhaps from a room in your house.

Found items

Chance finds can make interesting patio features, for example a pile of unusual stones, a scattering of shells, a few fossils or a heap of driftwood.

Sculptures

A single statue, a group of figures, or even a collection of amusing gnomes will all provide a focus of interest.

Ironwork

Decorative and functional ironwork items – such as shelf brackets, candle holders, screens, old farm and garden tools, and containers – can be hung on walls. There are many possibilities for adding an unusual flourish.

ORNAMENTS YOU CAN BUY

A patio without ornament is like an empty room – a rather sad place. However, a thoughtfully planned patio should not look cluttered – be selective when choosing ornaments, and don't be tempted to fill the patio until it is bulging with items that you don't really want or need. Start with just a few core items and proceed from there.

↗ *A patio is the perfect place for displaying sculpture. The huge choice of figurative items includes angels, classical figures, gnomes, pixies, rabbits, dogs, cats and pigs; abstract items encompass glass, ceramic, concrete or metal spheres and cones, stone and metal cubes.*

↗ *A small, self-contained water feature will enliven a tiny patio. You have a choice between abstract and figurative.*

↗ *Ceramic pots often look so good that they can be regarded more as pieces of sculpture than functional containers – there is a vast choice from plain to glazed in a range of colors; there are also some huge feature pots that can host a stunning display.*

↗ *Real fossils always look good – the Victorians displayed them in their walled gardens. Today you can also buy good imitations.*

↗ *Ironwork suits patios. Balusters, furniture, brackets, plant supports and rose arches contribute a rustic feel.*

↗ *Standing stones were once rare and expensive, but are now easy to buy. They make a perfect patio centerpiece.*

MAKE YOUR OWN ART AND SCULPTURE

A leaping fish design made from pieces of broken bathroom tile and crockery stuck on with tile cement.

Making patio art and sculptures is a wonderfully stimulating and therapeutic opportunity that should not be missed. Even if you are a novice, remember that the pleasure you derive from the process is equally as important as the finished results.

Mosaic pictures for patio walls

Mosaics are easy – just draw out the design, use a suitable waterproof adhesive or tile cement to stick down small pieces of glass tile, ceramic tile or broken pottery to make up the design, and then fill the joints with a waterproof grout. Clean excess grout off the surface before it dries.

Slate urns and creative shapes

Old roofing slate is a great material for building abstract sculptures. Decide on the form you want to create and draw it to size. Cut a template out of card or plywood, to follow the profile of the walls of the item. Build the walls with slate and mortar to the desired shape. Keep using the template to check that the side profile is correct. When the form is nearly finished, complete by using mortar to hold the slate in place.

An urn made by building slate walls according to a template profile.

Found objects

When it comes to decorative found objects, anything goes – one man's junk is another man's patio art.

Natural ~ Found objects from nature are wonderful and uniquely beautiful – rocks, shells, driftwood, bundles of twigs, stones covered in lichen, tree bark, stones pierced with holes, fossils, bleached bones, and pieces of wood that have been shaped by wind and rain.

Man-made ~ If you like old car wheel hubs, rusty buckets, discarded farm tools or old chimney pots, now is your chance to start a collection.

DON'T FORGET SAFETY

If you intend to display items such as farm implements, remember that they might be dangerous, especially in the hands of children. Render them harmless by fixing them beyond reach on a wall, or enclose them in some way so that inquisitive fingers are unable to explore.

Ponds

Is a patio a good place to have a pond?

Ponds are uniquely fascinating structures and can form a symbiotic relationship with a patio. A pond can be built on an existing patio or alongside it, to a sunken or raised design. It can contain a fountain, fish or plants. A pond always excites interest, and can liven up a space that is pleasant but unremarkable.

STYLE, SHAPE AND SIZE

If you want to create a small, easy-to-build pond – geometrical or irregular – without disturbing the integrity of the patio, it is best to build a raised pond that sits on the patio. Conversely, if you want a large pond, don't mind disturbing the surface of the patio, and are prepared for lots of work digging a hole and mixing concrete, create a sunken pond flush with the ground.

Measure your patio and consider a shape, size and style for the proposed pond. Visit a water garden center to look at examples.

Ponds have to be lined in order to hold water. The most common methods are either to use a pre-formed rigid liner or a sheet of flexible butyl rubber.

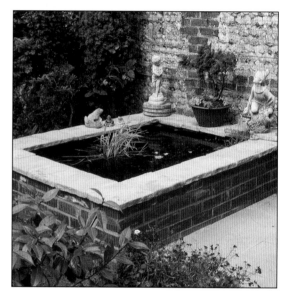

↗ *A partially sunken pond built from rendered concrete blocks with mosaic designs applied.*
→ *A raised pond made of brick with a coping of reconstituted stone slabs. It has a rigid liner.*

POND OPTIONS

POND LININGS

There are three methods of ensuring that a pond holds water. You can use a pre-formed plastic or resin liner, a flexible liner, or lay concrete.

Rigid lining ~ Pre-formed rigid liners look tempting in their simplicity, but they are expensive, small, and surprisingly tricky to fit. Resin ones last longer than those made of polypropylene.

Flexible lining ~ If you want to build a pond to your own design – to any size – a flexible liner is the best choice. Top-quality butyl lining will last a lifetime. Two layers of geo-textile will protect it from being pierced by stones.

Concrete lining ~ If you enjoy hard work and want a long-lasting pond at the lowest possible cost, concrete is the traditional answer.

Raised pond

Sunken pond

↑ A very simple raised pond built into the corner of an existing patio, matching an existing brick wall. The edge of the pre-formed rigid liner has been covered by the top row of bricks.
↗ A small, square, formal sunken pond with a stone paver edging, built as the central feature within an existing patio. The double-thickness concrete block wall has been rendered with mortar and brushed with waterproof pond paint.

Fish and plants

Fish ~ There is a choice: you can either introduce fish, or you can let native wildlife take over and wait for frogs, newts and suchlike to appear. You cannot easily have both.

Plants ~ The primary object of planting a pond is to achieve a "balance" between the amounts of oxygen and algae in the water. This ensures clear, sweet water.

HOW TO BUILD A RAISED POND

Using a flexible liner

↘ A raised pond can be built to any shape you wish by constructing a brick cavity ring wall on a concrete slab, with a flexible butyl liner laid across the base (and then running up between the cavity walls). A thin layer of concrete is spread over the base to protect the liner.

Using a rigid liner

↘ A pre-formed rigid liner is put in position on a concrete slab, and a brick ring wall built around it. The lip of the liner rests on the wall. The space between the inner face of the wall and the liner is packed with sand to give additional support to the liner.

Step 5
Cut the coping tiles to fit, so that they bridge the two walls and trap the liner, and bed them on mortar.

Step 4
Where the liner exits the cavity wall, cut away the protective textile to reveal the butyl. Fold it towards the pond and trim flush with the edge of the wall.

Step 3
Float 2 in of concrete over the liner.

Step 2
Lay the butyl across the foundation sandwiched between geo-textile and build the cavity wall. (The butyl is sandwiched between the two walls and the top edge is trapped under the coping tiles.)

Step 1
Dig a 12 in-deep foundation. Fill it with 6 in compacted gravel and 6 in concrete.

Step 4
Spread mortar on top of the walls and bed the coping tiles in place.

Step 3
Position the liner on the slab and build a double-thickness brick wall around it, filling the cavity between the liner and the wall with sand as you go.

Step 2
Dig the foundation to a depth of 12 in, then fill it with 6 in of compacted gravel and cover with 6 in of concrete. (The central area will contain sand to support the liner.)

Step 1
Calculate the size of the foundation and mark it on the ground with stakes and string.

HOW TO BUILD A SUNKEN POND

Buy a circular paving kit of reconstituted stone slabs. Dig the hole and spread a sandwich of geo-textile, butyl and geo-textile over the site. Cast a concrete slab in the bottom of the hole, on top of the geo-textile. Build a brick wall on the slab. The liner runs up the outside of the wall; pack sand between the sandwich and the sides of the hole. Top with hardcore, sand and the paving.

Step 5
Spread 2–4 in of compacted gravel over the site. Top with 2–4 in of sand.

Step 3
Fil the space between the outer layer of geo-textile and the hole with fine earth or sand.

Step 1
Dig a hole – depth to suit. Lay the butyl, sandwiched between geo-textile. Cast a concrete slab on top (6 in thick).

Step 6
Lay the slabs on blobs of mortar, with the edging lapping over the edge of the pond.

Step 4
Trim both sheets of geo-textile level with the top of the wall, and fold the butyl over and in towards the pond.

Step 2
Build a circular wall on the concrete slab, to finish up about 4 in below ground level.

FOUNTAINS, PUMPS AND FILTERS

If you want a fountain in the pond, you will need to fit a pump. If you are going to have a formal pond with a few plants and fish, you will need a pump and filter. These have to be planned at an early stage, so that water pipes and power cables can be hidden from view.

For example, the sunken pond opposite would need two pipes (one for water and the other to protect the power cable) running from the inside of the pond, through the bottom of the wall, up between the outside of the wall and the geo-textile, over the top of the wall and under the patio paving. All you will see is the pump and filter at the bottom of the pond.

For a raised pond, the best you can do is to disguise the piping. The pump sits in the bottom of the pond, the water pipe and the cable run up the inside of the pond and over the top edge, where you discreetly try to hide them under the coping, pebbles or perhaps a well placed plant.

Small water features

Can I have a feature with moving water on my patio?

A small water feature can transform a patio from a mere place to park a chair into a haven where you can enjoy the delightful sounds of water trickling, bubbling or gushing. There are lots of small, self-contained water features that do not involve building a pond; some do not even require the effort of digging a hole. Container ponds bring all the charms of a full-size pond, with a lot less effort. Visit a water garden center to look at all the possibilities on offer.

OPTIONS FOR SMALL WATER FEATURES

Container ponds

↗ A container pond can be made in anything from a large, ceramic pot to a wooden half-barrel. Just fill it with water, and add a few aquatic plants such as hornwort or irises. Another idea is to group a collection of containers, each of which is planted with different species.

Bubble fountains

↗ Bubble fountains consist of a fountainhead and a sump pump (or reservoir), which is set above or below ground. This is covered by your choice of feature, such as a millstone or pebbles. The pump pushes the water up through the fountainhead to run over the display before seeping back into the sump pump. This is an attractive, low-cost option.

Wall mask waterspout

↗ A wall mask waterspout gushes water into a reservoir pool at the base. A pump is placed in the reservoir, and connected to a delivery pipe that runs up the back of the wall and through the mask. To make life easier, an existing wall is preferable.

A ready-made water feature, which just needs to be filled with water and plugged in. It is attractive and safe, and children will love it. Together with many similar designs, it is available at a reasonable cost.

Container ponds

A container pond is no more than a container that holds water, so there are many suitable candidates. Here are some ideas, but you can also use many unusual items creatively.

Oak half-barrel ~ Wooden half-barrels make attractive containers. Soak them in water until the staves swell up and the barrel becomes watertight. The genuine article is preferable to reproductions.

Glazed ceramic pots ~ It is possible to buy ceramic pots in all shapes and sizes. Get the biggest that you can find. Drainage holes will have to be plugged with corks.

Galvanized water tank ~ Old galvanized house water supply tanks make capacious container ponds. They take on a special charm when full of water and an interesting range of plants.

Lead tank ~ These are quite difficult to find, but look imposing. Try searching in junkyards and at architectural salvage companies.

This old stone trough has great character and makes a stunning container pond.

Galvanized buckets and baths ~ Galvanized buckets, baths, troughs, watering cans and cattle feeders look great – the bigger and older the better.

HOW TO BUILD A BUBBLING URN FEATURE

↘You need a plastic container for the reservoir, a ceramic pot or urn (shape and size to suit), a small pump, about 3 yds of water delivery pipe, a sheet of wire mesh and a bucket of cobbles.

Dig a hole and set the container in place. Put the pump in it and protect the cable by passing it through a length of water pipe. Fit the water delivery pipe on to the pump outlet and run it out of the container. Cover the container with mesh, sit the urn in place, and disguise the mesh with cobbles.

A bubbling millstone water feature uses an identical hole, reservoir and pump set-up to the urn water feature.

Step 5
Fill the urn and the container with water. Switch on the power.

Step 4
Cover the mesh and pipes with a display of rocks and cobbles, so that the pipes are hidden.

Step 3
Cover the container with wire mesh and set the urn in position on top of it. Run the water delivery pipe into the urn.

Step 2
Put the pump in the reservoir and protect the cable with a length of water pipe. Connect the water delivery pipe to the pump.

Step I
Dig a hole to take the container. Set it in place with sand packed all around it.

HOW TO BUILD A WALL MASK WATERSPOUT

If you have an existing patio with a concrete foundation and a brick wall at one side, you can have a wall mask waterspout. Build a brick reservoir to match the wall (or use a ready-made trough or tank). Drill a hole through the wall, just above the brim of the reservoir, for the water pipe and the power cable. Drill a second hole where the mask is to hang. Sit the pump in the reservoir, and run the cable through the wall. Connect the ends of the water pipe to the pump and mask. Fill the reservoir with water and switch on.

Step 4
Fix the mask to the wall. Run the water pipe up the back of the wall and push it through the upper hole and the mask. At the back of the wall, fit plastic trunking to protect the water pipe and cable from damage.

Step 5
Fill the reservoir to the brim with clean water. Set the pump flow to suit and switch on.

Step I
Build a brick reservoir at the base of the wall (finish the inside with concrete and coat with pond paint); alternatively obtain a stone trough or a metal tank.

Step 3
Sit the pump in the reservoir and run the cable and water pipe through the hole. Drill another hole in the wall at the point where you want the mask to go.

Step 2
Drill a hole through the wall, just above the reservoir, big enough to take the water pipe and the pump cable.

PUMP POWER

The greater the head height (vertical distance from water surface to fountainhead) and spray height, the higher the flow rate needed. To calculate a pump's flow rate, time how long it takes to fill a container of known capacity – if it takes ten minutes to fill 100 liters, the flow rate is 10 liters per minute.

Flow rate in litres per hour

| 8820 |
| 8340 |
| 3800 |
| 3300 |
| 2760 |
| 1980 |

61 70 86 104 169 200
Pump power in watts

ELECTRICITY AND SAFETY

- *Always fit a circuit breaker between the pump and the power supply, to protect yourself from electric shock.*

- *Make sure that the electrics (all cables and sockets) are designed for outside use.*

- *It is good practice to avoid putting your hands in the water when the power is on, even if there is a circuit breaker.*

Barbecues

Is it safe to have a barbecue on a patio?

Patios and barbecues make perfect partners. There is something extremely enjoyable about eating out of doors – what could be better, on a warm summer's evening, than to light the barbecue, cook a meal, and then sit back and relax on the patio. If you wish, you can build in a barbecue as a permanent feature.

Safety

Barbecues are potentially dangerous. Always follow the manufacturer's directions. Never leave a barbecue unattended, never pour lighter fluids on a barbecue that appears to have gone out, and always be on your guard if your have young children.

BARBECUE OPTIONS

Built-in barbecue

↗ *A built-in brick barbecue makes an attractive patio feature. Consider carefully where you want it sited.*

Charcoal barbecues

↗ *There is something special about lighting and using a charcoal barbecue – it imparts a back-to-nature feel to cookery.*

Gas barbecue

↗ *If you would prefer to avoid the rituals of using a charcoal barbecue, a gas barbecue is a problem-free alternative.*

Disposable barbecue

↗ *A disposable barbecue is a great idea when there isn't room for a permanent set-up. It also avoids the need to buy charcoal.*

BEST POSITION

If you are planning to build a barbecue on the patio, think carefully about where to put it. Take into account safety aspects in relation to items such as decking and curtains. Assess the distance from the proposed barbecue to the table for suitability. Consider the direction of prevailing winds. Will the site will upset your neighbors?

When you have chosen a promising site, have a trial run by setting up a table to represent the barbecue. See what it feels like walking backwards and forwards from the "barbecue" to where you will be sitting. If you need a power source, consider how you are going to safely route the cable.

WINTER STORAGE

Portable charcoal, gas and electric barbecues, and the trays and grills of brick barbecues, need to be stored away in winter, ideally in a dry and well ventilated shed or garage.

Clean trays and grills before packing them away, and store gas bottles, fuel and charcoal as recommended by the manufacturer. Clean all barbecue tools before putting them away.

HOW TO BUILD A BRICK BARBECUE

Search out a DIY barbecue kit complete with a charcoal tray, cooking grill and fixings. The kit will tell you how many standard bricks are required. You also need a bag of mortar mix, a carpenter's level, a set square, a tape measure, a small trowel, a plastic bucket, and a piece of board about 1 yd square. Use a piece of chalk to mark out your chosen site. Mix the mortar on the board as directed, and dampen the bricks with water.

Step 5
When the mortar has partially set, use a trowel to tidy up the mortar and also to rake a little mortar from all the joints.

Step 4
Continue until you reach the recommended height. Push the metal support strips into the mortar joints.

Step 3
Spread mortar on the first course of bricks and bed the second course of dampened bricks in place.

Step 1
Brush the site clear of debris. Do a trial placing of the first and second courses of bricks, so you know what goes where.

Step 2
Dampen the bricks, spread mortar and bed the first course in place. Use a carpenter's level to test for vertical and horizontal alignment.

Lighting and heating

The sun may have gone down, but that doesn't mean you have to abandon the patio and go indoors. It is possible to enjoy your patio until late at night, and it can take on a new persona as a romantic or dramatic venue for entertaining. There are all manner of lights available, from electric to gas, or those based on candles. If it is late in the season and the air is getting nippy, there are wood and charcoal burners, or gas heaters, to make the patio comfortable.

How do I get maximum use out of my patio?

Planning lighting and heating for a new patio

Getting professional advice ~ If you are building a new patio from scratch and you know that you will want electric lighting and heating, plan out the position of the items and build ducting, sockets and supports into the design. Unless you are very confident about your proficiency, this is one of those times when it is best to bring in a professional to help, advise and do the tricky bits.

LIGHTING OPTIONS

General lighting ~ Available lighting ranges from genuine antique street lights to subtle uplighters and downlighters, and lights that illuminate the whole patio. Avoid lights that shine into your eyes. Low-voltage lights are a quick and easy option.

Table lighting ~ Table lights are designed to cast light on the eating area. Small candle lanterns are easy on the eyes and great for setting a mood.

Lighting for effect ~ Lights can add interest and excitement to a patio. Try party lights, Christmas lights, Chinese lanterns or coach lights. Spotlights can be used to highlight plants or a water feature.

A modern globe light

A pretty candle lantern

Patio heaters

Gas and electric heaters are certainly instant and efficient (within a radius of a couple of yards), but nothing is quite so dynamic as a traditional woodburning stove with a chimney. The drawback is that it can be difficult to light, smoky, and needs watching. On the plus side, a stove makes an exciting addition.

General lighting

General lighting for the patio is much the same as general lighting in the home – it consists of straightforward overhead or wall lights that illuminate a space.

You need one or more of these no-nonsense lights around the patio area. Small wall lights are a good option – they are relatively inexpensive and easy to install. If your patio is remote from the house and without walls, use standard lights or tree lights.

Lighting for effect

General lights are ideal for illuminating a whole area, but you need smaller lights in order to create a mood or effect. There are lots of options. You can have strings of little colored lights, lanterns, lights half-buried in the ground, high-tech solar lights, spirit torches that are spiked in the ground, scented candles, and so on.

There are two safety issues to take into account – children and candles are a bad mix, and strong flashing lights are not good for people who are partially sighted or who suffer from migraines.

Table lighting

If you are planning an after-dark dinner party, the table needs to be lit in some way. There are many electric lights to choose from, but the drawback of a power cable is that it is unsightly and presents a potential trip hazard. It is much better to deck your table with an assortment of lanterns, or tea lights in colored glass jars – the flickering shadows they create look wonderful.

Protect yourself by using a circuit breaker

For safety's sake, all garden electrics need to be fitted with a GFCI or Ground Fault Circuit Interrupter. This inexpensive and completely necessary device ensures that the power is instantly cut off if the cable is damaged by accident.

Index